THE
LIGHT
WITHIN
YOU

OTHER BOOKS BY JOHN CLAYPOOL

Tracks of a Fellow Struggler
Stages: The Art of Living the Expected
The Preaching Event: The Lyman Beecher Lectures

THE LIGHT WITHIN YOU

John R. Claypool

WORD BOOKS
PUBLISHER
WACO, TEXAS

A DIVISION OF
WORD, INCORPORATED

THE LIGHT WITHIN YOU
LOOKING AT LIFE THROUGH NEW EYES

Library of Congress Cataloging in Publication Data:

Claypool, John.
  The light within you.

  1. Christian life—Baptist authors. I. Title.
BV4501.2.C559   1983   248.4'86132   83–3578
ISBN 0-8499-0273-8

Printed in the United States of America

First Printing, May 1983
Second Printing, November 1983

To my wife, Ann,
whose love and warmth
and light within
make life and ministry
a joyous sharing

CONTENTS

FOREWORD

Nineteen sixty-four was the year of my passage from—
Chicago to Colorado Springs,
from
a secular job to Young Life,
from
death into life.

It was also the year I began reading John Claypool's printed sermons—first from a Louisville church . . . then from a Fort Worth church . . . and finally from a Jackson (Mississippi) church.

Great is the power of the written word, for in those sermons I found answers to deep longings that my new faith was posing.

For eighteen years I gleaned the very secrets of God from John's Sunday messages to his congregations. How I grew and flourished in my understanding of God and myself!

Three questions have plagued me for the better part of my fifty years:

- Who is God?
- Who am I?
- What is my life all about?

And as I have talked with people across the years, I have begun to realize that I have a lot of company with these concerns. These questions seem to be at the base of our being; they have challenged people down through the ages. The struggle for meaning, for identity, is our unending quest from the very beginning.

John Claypool brought God to me in words and terms that I could understand . . . and answers to those three questions slowly began to come into focus. *I was excited!* And when one is in that state, *he leaps for joy,* and shouts, "I was blind . . . but now I see."

That's exactly what I did with my wife, Carol, and the Young Life staff. I blitzed them with John's sermons over the years . . . so that these truths have now shaped and molded my family as well as the Young Life mission. How privileged we have been!

A few years ago, God moved in my heart to put together a manuscript of these sermons for possible publication—as an expression of gratitude to John Claypool, and to make it possible for others to share in the Good News that "God loves us . . . and we are free to live." I spread out eighteen years of John's sermons (approximately eight hundred) on the floor and began to select the ones that would tell this story in a careful order. I know them all by heart, so it was an easy task. The twenty-two sermons (now rewritten into chapters) are the result of that selection process.

These truths, as interpreted by John Claypool, have transformed my very life for Christ Jesus' sake. And they will do that to yours, also!

The world still waits to know the God of Abraham, Isaac, and Jacob. This book will reveal his true nature . . . and his immense love for each of us!

BILL TAYLOR
Secretary and Treasurer
Young Life International

PREFACE

In many ways, this book is different from any other I have written, and you the reader are entitled to know this from the outset. The chapters that follow were not originally formulated at one sitting as organic units of a single project. They were first created as sermons preached in three different congregational settings over a period of fifteen years.

In a real sense, Bill Taylor is primarily responsible for this collection of insights. Through our mutual friend Bob Rice, Bill began receiving copies of my sermons by mail back in the 1960s. He was the one who culled through many offerings and suggested the specific ones that are found here. I remain profoundly moved and grateful that Bill took my work so seriously and went to the trouble of formulating this proposal.

Another acknowledgment of thanks needs to go to Floyd Thatcher at Word Books for blessing the idea and giving me the go-ahead. The project languished for several months, and then Anne Christian Buchanan entered the picture as editor and did a tremendous amount of work in moving the material from a sermonic to a more literary form of being. Traces of "the former life" are still evident, but much of the credit for arrangement, compacting, and clarifying the book go to this careful and perceptive young editor.

11

PREFACE

Thus, many heads and hands and hearts collaborated to produce the following pages. In the final analysis, only God is capable of true originality and exclusive creativity. The rest of us simply pass on some of what we have been given ("what do you have you did not receive?") and do this rearranging in concert and with the help of countless others. Therefore, gratitude is much more appropriate than pride in relation to any project in which we humans are involved.

These are the folk who helped me specifically with this particular book. I need to say one last word of general thanks to my wife, Ann. She came into my life at a time of great pain and deadness and near despair. Her gift— love—more than any other human factor, was used by God to call me back to life and hope again. Without her, this project would have "died in the wilderness" long ago. That it comes to be now is another evidence of the resurrection-reality that is the only and final hope for any of us.

May whatever light exists in these pages warm and illumine all of you who touch it!

JOHN CLAYPOOL
Lubbock, Texas
January, 1983

THE
LIGHT
WITHIN
YOU

1

SHAPING YOUR ASSUMPTIONS

Mark 1:24–26; Genesis 3:1–7

WHEN I WAS ABOUT TEN YEARS OLD, a deacon in my home church who was also an official of the city was indicted on the charge of embezzling a large sum of public money. The papers on Saturday were full of this story; therefore, it was not surprising that the scandal was the main topic of conversation at church the next day. As I listened to the "big people" talk, I heard two very different reactions to this single event. Some people said, "I simply don't believe it. I've known that man for forty years and he is not a crook. This is just a trumped-up political smear." However, other people said, "I wasn't surprised at all when I read the papers yesterday. I never have trusted that man. There is something about him that has always made me suspicious."

I remember being confused by these differing reactions, for I did not yet realize just how complex the human decision-making process can be. Obviously, in this case, more was involved than just an objective re-

15

sponse to bare facts. Before the man was ever accused of anything, people had evidently formed certain impressions of him, and these prior assumptions explain why one person could look at the situation and say, "I don't believe it; there must be some mistake," while another person could look at the same set of facts and say, "I'm not surprised at all. I never have trusted that backslapper from the first."

This early experience taught me a lesson I have never forgotten—that our assumptions are all-important when it comes to how we deal with the facts in the world around us. We are not purely rational, objective creatures. What we end up with as a conclusion is going to be deeply colored by what we begin with as an assumption, and this applies as much to our relationship with God as it does to any other aspect of our existence. The crucial thing here is not simply what God does or does not do in history, but whether our starting point is one of trust or mistrust. That beginning assumption can make all the difference.

I experienced this truth firsthand several years ago in Kentucky when I went to the hospital to see about a man who had just undergone surgery. I met his wife and sister in the surgical recovery waiting room, where they had just been told he was filled with cancer and probably had only a few weeks to live. This terrible news was made all the more painful by the fact that the man had just retired after a distinguished career and had been making all kinds of plans with his wife for this new phase of their life.

All three of us were overcome at first by the bad news, but then his wife said quietly, "I'm not going to pass judgment on this until God gets through with it. We have no idea what may come of this situation. Things may not be as bad as the surgeon thinks. There may be an act of healing, or some unexpected form of good may result from Henry's illness. It's too soon to tell just now. The goodness and mercy of God have followed us all the days of our lives, and he will not forsake us now. Like Job said, 'Though it seems like he is slaying me, yet will I trust him.' "

I was awed by this magnificent statement of faith in a difficult situation, and I was reaching out my hand to commend the woman when the man's sister literally exploded in rage at both of us. She screamed, "How can you pietists talk like that? Can't you see from all this that God must be some kind of sadist? This world is nothing but a torture chamber, one big cruelty joke. I can see God now, splitting his sides in laughter over what he's pulled on poor Henry. Here he has worked all his life, looking forward to retirement, and now what happens? Four weeks to the day and he is put on the rack of cancer. And all of this came from those same wonderful folks who give us tornadoes and hurricanes and epidemics! I'm not at all surprised that this has happened. It's just like God to get your hopes up and then dash them to pieces."

Needless to say, the contrast between the women who stood on either side of me was awesome. And it was clear that in that moment the same thing was happening that had taken place in the halls of my home church years ago. A single event had led to diametrically opposite responses. Why? Because the assumptions with which each of the women began had drastically colored the conclusions to which she came. Across the years, one had come to think trustingly of the Almighty, so that she said, "I'll wait to pass judgment until God is finished with all this; some good will undoubtedly come out of it." The other woman had somehow come to distrust God, and her reaction was: "It's just like him, the sadistic old killjoy!"

You see, assumptions are absolutely crucial—which leads to the question, How do we go about forming these powerful realities? By what process do we build up these impressions that become so influential in shaping our decisions?

According to the Bible, this is the place where trouble often begins—we do not take the task of assumption building seriously enough. We tend to be sloppy, irrational, and arbitrary in this area of our lives, with the result that our whole decision-making mechanism is thrown out of kilter. Jesus said, "Your eye is the lamp of your body. When your eyes are good, your whole body also is full of light. But when they are bad, your body also is full of darkness. See to it, then, that the light within you is not darkness" (Luke 11:34–35, NIV). He was talking about the process of constructing our basic assumptions and about the care with which we go about that process. Do we base our assumptions on solid evidence or arbitrary hearsay?

The book of Genesis describes how the first mistrust of God came to exist, and it is a classic example of careless, irrational assumption building. Out of the joy of his own aliveness, God decided to create the world. He had no ulterior motives for this; he was not trying to get something for himself. Rather, he was trying to give something of himself—to widen the circle of joy—and this is why everything got called out of nonbeing into existence. Having set this experiment of joy into motion, he proceeded to show the man and the woman how things were meant to work. They were free to eat from all the trees of the Garden except one—the Tree of the Knowledge of Good and Evil. The fruit of this tree was poisonous to their systems, God said, and had been placed there to serve a religious rather than a nutritional purpose. God was obviously excited about what he had done. The whole mechanism looked good—in fact "very good"—to his generous eyes.

Then, out of nowhere, a snake moved into the picture and began to ask questions. He said to the woman, "Did God put you down in this beautiful place and then prohibit you from eating all this fruit?" She corrected him quickly, for that was a gross overstatement. She replied, "Oh no, we can eat everything in the garden except that tree in the center, which God said would be poisonous to us."

At that point the serpent began to shake his head and said, "The old scoundrel. He is threatened by you, you know. He realized that if you eat that fruit you will be just like him, and he could not stand that. He has created you to bolster his own ego. Holding you down builds him up. If you stupid slaves knew what was good for you, you would call his bluff. You'd eat that fruit and take over this place and be done with all this over-under stuff."

Such talk must have startled the wits out of the first humans, for it put the drama of creation in a wholly different light. There is no indication that suspicion of this sort had ever entered their minds before. More important, there was not one shred of evidence for such an attitude of distrust! Nothing God had ever done would have given the humans reason to believe the serpent's accusations, and this is the tragedy of it all. Without really checking things out or going to the Source and trying to get to the bottom of the situation, the first man and woman carelessly bought into that unfounded suspicion. For no good reason, they embraced rumor and began to act as if it contained the truth about God. What incredible carelessness, and what devastating results.

What would you think of me if I got sick and tried to medicate myself for awhile, until my illness grew so bad that finally I had to call my trusted family doctor? Suppose, when he came out to examine me, that I showed him the medicine I had been taking, and he said, "That is the worst possible stuff for your problem. Put it away and start taking this prescription I will give you. In a matter of hours, I promise, you will start feeling better."

19

Then, when the doctor left, suppose a plumber who was unstopping my sink came out and said, "I overheard that conversation. Did that doctor tell you to quit taking your old medicine and start taking some of this new stuff? . . . Those mercenary doctors! The problem is your old medicine was paid for and there was no profit in it for him. The only reason he is giving you this new prescription is to make some more shekels. You can't trust an M.D. these days. If you know what is good for you, you will stick with the medicine you have already paid for and forget all about that new prescription."

Now I ask you, what would you think of me if I bought into that kind of mistrust? Would you not say I was crazy to take the word of a plumber over that of a trusted physician when it comes to medicine? Yet, according to Genesis, this is exactly what our forbears did back in the beginning. They took the word of a snake over the word of their Creator when it came to interpreting life! They uncritically accepted a negative image of God that had no basis in fact, and look at what has resulted from that one erroneous assumption! Thinking the world was a conspiracy rather than a creation and God a foe rather than a father, the humans proceeded to take life apart and put it together in ways that did not work. They drank the poison and got sick, just as they had been warned, and all of creation proceeded to degenerate into chaos.

This is how God's bad reputation got started—with a flimsy accusation by a snake and some sloppy, careless assumption work—and it has been a problem in history ever since. Jesus ran into it that day he went into the synagogue and the man with the unclean spirit cried out, "Have you come to destroy us? I know who you are, the Holy One of God" (Mark 1:24). Here was the ancient suspicion of the serpent, accepted and acted upon. I ran into the same thing that day in the hospital as the sick man's sister railed out against the cruelty of a sadistic God. And

I myself am no stranger to such feeling patterns. My earliest impressions of the Almighty were tinged with negativism. I thought when one said, "Thy will be done," one was asking for suffering and agony; to obey God was to say goodbye to joy and pleasure. In fact, I think this is the assumption most people have accepted down at the bottom of their beings. Since those beginning days, to use a modern phrase, God has suffered from a bad press.

And how do you suppose God responded to this carelessness-that-led-to-error-that-led-to-chaos, this unmaking of his beautiful world? The miracle is that he did not blow up in rage; that would have been understandable. Neither did he become defensive and strike back in anger. No, according to the Bible, his response was the single most creative thing he could have done: "He . . . spared not his own Son, but delivered him up for us all" (Rom. 8:32, KJV).

As John Killinger once put it, "Jesus is God's way of getting rid of a bad reputation." Who is this Jesus? To use a West Texas phrase, he is "the spittin' image" of his Father. And he became what we are—a flesh and blood human being—so we could understand what he is. Over against all the confusion and suspicion that had been generated by the ages, God sent his only begotten Son so that people could see what he looked like in history, walking the streets of a city in wide-open daylight. And the question became: Can you trust a God like that? Is the One this Jesus portrays really a sadist, trying to hold people down and dehumanize them, or is he the joyful Creator who all along had nothing but good in mind?

Jesus was God's attempt to set right what had really gone wrong—our basic assumptions about him. This is why Paul could say of all this, "God was in Christ, reconciling the world unto himself" (2 Cor. 5:19, KJV). Jesus was God's way of reaching all the way down to our assumption level and showing us that, from the Garden on, we have been mistaken about who he is and what he wants to do with us.

But the question is, Are you willing to take this action of God seriously enough to let it do its work? I promise you, if you will allow the image of Jesus to penetrate down to the level of your assumptions, your whole outlook can be changed. And I ask you, if you can't trust a Christlike God, who can you trust? Imagine what would happen if you were to faint away in the presence of Jesus of Nazareth and become totally vulnerable and defenseless. On the basis of what you see of him in the New Testament, what do you think he would do to you? Would he steal your money, exploit your body, take advantage of your helplessness? Of course not! Of all the people in the world, who could you trust more to help and not hurt you? And the Good News is that this one is the visible image of the invisible God! What Jesus was during the days of his flesh, God has always been and will always be.

Therefore, when it comes to making up your assumptions about the Holy One, for his sake and for yours, do it carefully and realistically. As the old saying goes, "When you're sick, see a doctor, not a plumber." And when it comes to understanding God, listen to his Son, not to some dumb snake. Killinger is right; "Jesus is God's way of getting rid of a bad reputation." The question is, have you let him do his reconciling work in you?

2

THE ORIGINS OF ALIENATION

Genesis 3:1–8

A HUNDRED YEARS FROM NOW—if humankind is still alive on this planet—historians may look back on our growing consciousness of ecological problems as a real milestone in the human pilgrimage. In the past two decades, attention has been increasingly focused on the apocalyptic threat that now hangs over our planet in terms of what we are doing to our natural environment— to the air, to the water, to the earth. For many of us, this has represented the surfacing of a brand-new problem. We may never even have heard the word *ecology* a few years ago, and were conditioned to think that atomic destruction and racial warfare were the most imminent threats to the well-being of the twentieth century. Those specters still loom, but now yet another "horseman" has been added to the arsenal of anxiety—the possibilities of annihilation by suffocation or by starvation or by merely being trampled to death by too many people are being brought home with graphic urgency.

Now, obviously, this whole issue of the earth and its survival is of great religious significance, for if the Bible teaches us anything, it teaches us that this earth and its inhabitants are extremely important to God. What happens to us here makes a tremendous difference to him, because he made us and loves us and has already made a tremendous investment of himself in this planet. Therefore, to view all this concern for the environment as outside the domain of religion is to be about as unbiblical as one can be.

However, even saying that does not exhaust the religious implication of this subject, for the Bible has more than concern over environmental issues; it also has something to say about the *cause* of our problems with the environment. If you look deep into the heart of this situation and want to know how we humans ever got into these kinds of straits with our environment, you find yourself in the realm of ultimate relationships—how human beings connect with themselves and with God and with others and with the universe—and this happens to be a realm about which the Bible has a great deal to say. It is at this dimension of the problem that I want us to look now. You have probably had it "up to here" with facts and statistics about pollution and pesticides and population and all the rest, but as Christian people we need to get behind all these "whats" to the more basic "why." At bottom I feel the ecological problem is one of spirit—a matter of how human beings view themselves and relate to the world—and I believe that if creative solutions are to be found, they will be found at this level.

As a way to begin, I suggest we turn to one of the most influential books of this century, a long religious poem called *I And Thou* by the Jewish mystic Martin Buber. As you may already know, what Buber does is describe the two basic ways a human being can relate to life. The first of these is called an "I-Thou" relationship, and consists in openness and meeting and mutual sharing. The premise underneath this way of relating is the belief that all of creation is alive, and that we can approach anything with reverence and awe and so unite with it that it can disclose its secret to us and we can disclose our secret to it. Before I read this poem for myself—when I had only heard about it—I assumed the "I-Thou" relationship was limited to God and to other human beings, but this assumption was erroneous. Buber said—and this point is crucial for our discussion here—that one can also have this kind of relationship with material objects and animals! "I-Thou" is a way of being present to and transacting with the whole of creation. It is a thoroughly personal approach, for it means that we relate to whatever is beyond us with the sense that it too is alive and has something to give and receive.

The other kind of relationship Buber describes is what he calls the "I-It" relationship and this is a fundamentally different way for two entities to relate to one another. Here a split opens up between subject and object, and the sense of aliveness goes out of the relationship. Instead of the two meeting in mutuality, what happens is that one person sets himself or herself over against a person or an object, and then proceeds to analyze and categorize and use and manipulate that person or object. There is no dialogue or reciprocity here; "I-It" is a one-way transaction in which one does something *to* the other rather than *with* it. It is essentially an impersonal sort of relationship and, once again, it is a stance that can be adopted toward all of creation. We can choose to relate to another human being or even to God in the "I-It" pattern, just as surely as we can relate to a flower or a cat in the "I-Thou" pattern. How we relate to what is outside ourselves is mostly a matter of our inner attitude; we can be personally alive and open to the whole spectrum of reality—even the inorganic—or we can be impersonal and over against it all—even Divinity. In describing the human situation this way, I think Buber has done us a tremendous service, for his concepts make the early chapters of Genesis come alive with penetrating insight as to what life should be and what has happened to us.

For example, the first two chapters of this document make it clear that God created the world in an "I-Thou" fashion and meant for it to function that way. By the very assertion that God called all things into being by a word, the ancient writer is trying to say, "All things are capable of communicating with each other." We do not have sections of reality that are dead or inert in themselves. All things are alive with the life of God; all are shaped by a word; all things can thus be met in openness and can both give of themselves and receive. And, of course, human beings were set down in the midst of this mutuality and given the highest communication capacity of all— the ability to be personal with absolutely everything! The depiction of a human being walking with God in the cool of the day and naming the animals and tending the earth is a way of saying, "Creation is alive in its totality. Everything is connected up with everything else, and all share and interact in the rhythm of 'I-Thou' forever."

But then chapter three of Genesis describes an event of catastrophic proportions that exploded amid the finely balanced creation. It can be understood basically as a shift in relationship from "I-Thou" to "I-It." This was precisely what the serpent was trying to do—to get man and woman to pull out of the connectedness of creation and to set themselves over against all things, there to analyze and to observe and to use for themselves. Significantly enough, the serpent suggested that Adam and Eve make such a break first with God—that is, instead of sharing openly and honestly with him, to separate themselves and to analyze God's actions and motives in abstraction rather than in mutuality. I have often wondered how dif-

ferent the outcome would have been had the first humans taken their doubt to God within the context of their
relationship and asked him honestly if he were in fact trying to hold them down. In such mutuality, I imagine the
Father could have very adequately demonstrated his
goodness. But humankind did not choose to deal with
their doubt in this way. No, the momentous break in the
harmony of creation came when human beings decided
to turn God into an "It" and to decide for themselves in
isolation what he was doing.

In that moment the vital bond of connectedness was
torn asunder and the Genesis story depicts with frighten-
ing thoroughness how everything else began to fall apart
as a result of this basic shift. We hear a lot today about
"the domino theory" of cause and effect, in which one
movement sets off a chain reaction and "all these things
happen because that happened." Well, the movement of
humankind out of the circle of an "I-Thou" relationship
with God set off a chain reaction of unbelievable proportions. Before it was over, what had functioned in vital
harmony was shattered into the smithereens of alienation.

For example, man and woman became separated from
their own beings. They were suddenly ashamed of their
bodies, and began even to hide part of themselves from
themselves by means of clothes. They found themselves
cut off from God, the eternal Thou. They had once
walked together with God in the cool of the day and
known joyous oneness, but now they had to hide from
"The Great It" over against whom they had dared put
themselves. Alienation also became real between the man
and the woman; what they had decided together to do
had by no means united them. Under questioning, Adam
angrily tried to shift the blame for what had happened to
the woman, and thus set himself over against her. And
the same thing happened to their relationship with all the

natural realm. When the trees and the fruit had been approached as living "Thous" with whom one shared, an affectionate solidarity bound nature to humankind. But once these same objects became "Its"—things out there to take and eat and do with as one pleased—impersonally—all of that changed. Humankind's relation to the earth became a wearisome battle against a stubborn foe instead of a sharing with a loving mother.

In these powerful symbols, this ancient story makes clear not only *what* happened to human beings in the beginning of time, but also *why*, and nothing could be more relevant to the ecological crisis in which we find ourselves just now. How have we gotten into these straits, both with each other and the environment? At bottom, the answer is summed up in one word: *alienation*. We who were created for "I-Thou" relationships with the whole of reality have chosen to tear ourselves out of such living connectedness. We have become embattled over against everything else in an "I-It"—using, exploiting, manipulating—kind of relationship.

It is because things are like this with us at the spirit level that they are what they are at the environmental level. We have lost touch with who we are in relation to the earth, and with who the earth is in relation to us, and this is why we have been so brutal with nature, literally raping the earth as if it were something dead and worthless that we are free to push around, use, or throw away as we please. Another way of putting it is to say that, because we have lost the true way of being with the elements of the world, we have been driven to substitute quantity for quality and to make up with many things our lack of deep relationship with any one thing.

The late Samuel Miller was right on the point when he observed, shortly before his death, that we Americans are always accused of being materialistic and loving things too much, but that the very opposite is the case. "We

Americans do not love things enough," he said. "If we did, we would not have so many of them." It is true that real love is a selective and exclusive process. When you genuinely love something, you want to be with it, to spend time in its presence, and so to unite with it that it can show itself to you and you to it. To love deeply is to love exclusively. However, when one is incapable of such love, the most obvious subsititute is to love many things superficaly. A man who will not love one woman deeply and faithfully may try to make up for it by loving many women, but the emptiness is there. And what could be a more telling judgment of our American condition than our glut of affluence? We would not need so many things if we knew how really to love and appreciate any one thing the way it should be loved. But we do not, and this poverty of spirit is what is driving us madly into more and more affluence. This, in turn, is precisely what is causing the environmental crisis that now threatens us.

Do you realize just how wasteful and destructive our consumer-oriented, disposable approach to life really is? In 1969 alone our country produced forty-eight billion cans and twenty-eight billion bottles to be disposed of, not to mention the seven million cars that had to be junked or the one hundred and forty-two billion tons of pollution we sent into the atmosphere. A biologist at the University of Kentucky, Dr. Wayne Davis, estimates that we Americans are anywhere from twenty-five to five hundred times as destructive of our environment as was the average Indian, and that, as a result, we may be the first continent on the globe to perish without any land or air or water resources left!

The situation at the material level is indeed serious. But, I repeat, our material problems are rooted in another level of existence—the spiritual level, the source of how we relate to ourselves and to God and to others and to the world. All the turbulence at the ecological level finds its cause in what has happened on the spiritual plane of our existence.

Is there, then, any hope of a solution to so deep and complex a problem? The Bible certainly holds forth such, but understandably suggests that it must begin where the break first occurred—at the personal, spiritual level. What was the problem that led to the original alienation, when human beings wrenched themselves out of the living "I-Thou" relation with all things into the embattled "I-It"?

According to Genesis, alienation began with the fact that those human beings did not like themselves; they were not satisfied with who they were. The problem there was not one of pride, as if humans loved themselves too much. It had to have been the opposite, or they never would have been hooked by the particular temptation of the serpent. You see, had humans liked themselves, when the serpent said, "Look, you ought to eat of that tree, for then you could become like God," they would have been able to say, "But we don't want to be God: we're not divine. We're his children, and we like being who we are, thank you. We don't need to be anything different." Had Adam and Eve loved themselves, the temptation to alienation would not have succeeded, but they did not, so it did—and thus the problem.

The solution, then, has to start here, at this point of relating to self, if what has gone wrong is ever going to be set right. I know this may sound remote and inconsequential and maybe even seem like a throwback to individualistic piety, but I honestly believe this is "where it's at," to use a somewhat dated expression. The seeds of the ecological crisis are in every one of us, and if healing and change are ever going to come, they must begin with our own alienated hearts. Somehow people must be touched at this level of how they feel about themselves, for until that original breach of alienation is closed, all the other gaps will remain.

Let us not underestimate for one moment the depth of this problem of getting humans to love themselves. We all have so much self-despising ground into us by culture and experience and even religion that nothing short of "being born again" spiritually can change the cycle. Just recently I was talking to some people about the Good News that God loves who we are and wants us to be ourselves, and one man retorted angrily, "I don't buy all this talk about self-acceptance. I don't like myself. I never have. I want more than anything else to be something else." I tried to assure him that I understood his feelings, for I had felt that way most of my life. However, I went on to point out that nothing was really more heretical or blasphemous from a biblical point of view, for in effect what he was saying was, "God made a mistake when he made me. He did not know what he was doing when he called me into being." As we talked on, I think he began to realize for the first time who and what he was—a beloved and gifted creature of God—and he began to feel about himself the way Jesus Christ showed us God feels about every person. After all, grace has to begin with the first thing God ever did to us—the act of creating us— and until we accept it at that point, how can it work anywhere else? What needs to be done is what God has been trying to do ever since the terrible fall of humankind—to get humans to love themselves because he loves them and, out of such love, to connect up with everything else he has made out of love, and thus to know the vital harmony of an "I-Thou" relationship rather than the alienated stance of the "I-It" relationship.

As I see it, this is the most important contribution the church can make to the apocalyptic crisis in ecology. If health is ever going to return to the earth, what needs to be healed is that point where the sickness first entered. According to the Bible, that was us—humankind—and this mistaken notion about ourselves that as we are we are not OK, that we should be something else. The whole thrust of biblical truth is God's affirmation of who we are. He made us, likes us, wants us to be in relationship with all else he has made. And the only hope for this planet lies in letting him teach us to love ourselves, and from there to get in touch with him and with others and with the whole world of "the Thou."

Some people are saying it already may be too late. A century from now there may be no people alive on this planet Earth because of the sickness of alienation beginning with the self. But before we conclude that and give up, let us do our utmost to be part of the answer and not part of the problem. There are many ways to do this, but the place to start is beginning to love yourself as God loves you and all human beings. Then—in-season and out-of-season—you can begin to spread the word of God's love all around you. That may seem like the long way around, but believe me, it is the only way really to treat the real problem.

Start at Chapter ↓

3

OUR PEACE IS IN OUR PLACE

1 Samuel 11:5–15

SOME YEARS AGO I preached a series of sermons on the pivotal figures of Old Testament history under the general title, "Remembering Who We Are." The rationale back of this emphasis was that, in order for us to come to know ourselves adequately, we need to come to terms with the heritage that lies behind us, to have some understanding of how we have come to be what we are.

I remember engaging in this sort of process as a child. I used to look forward eagerly to Thanksgiving and Christmas, because the larger family would gather and there would always be reminiscing about our ancestors. All sorts of tales would be told about this and that forebear; it gave me a clearer sense of my own identity to hear about the many different people that made up my Buchanan and Claypool heritage. And what is significant in the family realm is also true in the religious sense. I am sure this is why the Old Testament was included as a part of the Holy Scriptures by the early church. There is no way

33

to understand Jesus of Nazareth and the events that grew out of his ministry apart from the long heritage of Judaism which the Old Testament recounts. This is our background, too, and one of the significant figures in that heritage is Saul, the first man to serve as king of the chosen people of Israel.

In order to understand this man, we will need to keep in mind the historical situation into which he was thrust as a young man. It had been some two hundred years since Israel had come out of Egypt and entered the land of promise. However, they were by no means a tightly organized people. They lived primarily as remotely related clans. Occasionally a crisis would arise and some hero like Gideon or Samson would unite Israel for a brief time, but there was no ongoing political structure among the twelve tribes. The God Yahweh was their only king, and they lived together at best in a loosely organized confederacy.

However, in the eleventh century B.C. a new threat emerged on the horizon. A people called the Philistines organized themselves under a king and developed a standing army that utilized metal weapons. The volunteer militias of the Hebrew clans were no match for this kind of force, and before long the Philistines had conquered the central plateau of Palestine and leveled Shiloh and turned much of Israel back into slavery. It was much like the contest between the organized White man and the simple Red man on our continent, and it was obvious that Israel's old ways were no longer adequate. The political structure that had served their first two hundred years could not meet this new challenge of organized aggression, and it is not surprising that a clamor arose in Israel to unite under a king.

It fell to Samuel's lot to help the children of Israel recognize this reality and "turn the corner" toward a new form of government. As we will see later, Samuel had

mixed feelings about such a move. He represented the
last of the "hero rulers" who had no constituted authority
but ruled by personal charisma. All his life had been invested in the old model of leadership. However, Samuel
was wise enough to realize that what had been adequate
for the days of his youth was not appropriate for the new
situation. So, under the leadership of Yahweh, he was
led to a handsome young man named Saul and proceeded to anoint him as Israel's very first king.

At that point in time, Saul appeared to have been the
perfect choice. He had all the gifts to seize this great opportunity and to become a stunning success. He came
from a well-to-do family that owned extensive property,
and he possessed outstanding leadership qualities. Saul
was physically impressive—literally a full head and
shoulders taller than the average Hebrew. He also had
the ability to inspire the confidence of other people and
to motivate them to act. For example, when the Ammo-
nites sought to take advantage of Israel's problems with
the Philistines and to further humiliate the Israelites, Saul
responded in indignation and aroused all Israel out of
their faintheartedness to battle against these ancient ad-
versaries. According to the writers of 1 Samuel, Saul "put
fresh heart" into his countrymen, and through his efforts
was able to roll back the Philistines from the central
plateau and establish Israel once again as master of the
beloved "Promised Land."

With all this active promise and brilliant beginning, it is
therefore startling to read that, in less than ten years,
Saul wound up a totally defeated man who took his own
life. Suicide is always an awesome phenomenon, especially when it comes at the end of a promising career.
One cannot help but ask: What happened in those ten
short years? How did the handsome young Saul so
quickly degenerate into a tragic suicide?

It is possible to formulate an answer to such a question

because the biblical record is surprisingly honest, even about its heroes. This is one thing that distinguishes it from other historical documents. Most ancient records were largely mythological; that is, they "hid the skeletons" and presented things in the best light. But the Bible does not do this. It is one of the earliest examples of "telling it like it is." Not even its greatest heroes are depicted as perfect. Therefore, we are able to piece together some of the factors that account for Saul's tragic demise. There is much for us to learn here besides information about one of our forebears—what happened to Saul could happen to any one of us. What then, did go wrong? Let me identify three factors.

First of all, the despair that settled over Saul at the end of his life may have developed partly out of the unrealistic expectations he had for the office of king. It is clear from all the accounts that Saul did not seek kingship for himself; in fact, he was very reluctant to assume the post. However, once it was thrust upon him, he did set out to do the job and to meet the challenges of the Philistines. But perhaps he dreamed too idealistically and failed to reckon with the slow pace and great agony that always characterize massive social change.

Let me underline once again the radical nature of the change Israel was undergoing. They had never had much internal organization. Their life in the Promised Land still bore marks of the independence that had characterized their life in the desert. There was much in their tradition to militate against a human king with ongoing authority. It was only the threat of the Philistines that led Samuel and the rest of Israel to create a new form of government, and they did so with great reluctance. Try to imagine what would occur if someone set out to establish a monarchy in America just now. Think of the conflict and opposition such a change would arouse! From the very beginning, this was exactly the sort of thing Saul encountered. It appears he was unprepared for such an ordeal and was discouraged by it.

This is a very typical mistake of the young. They often come up "from the gates in the morning" with bursting idealism and they want with "one fell swoop" to set right all that has gone wrong. Then they run headlong into the stubborn intransigence of the status quo and are quickly dismayed. Dr. Ernest Campbell tells us of encountering a young man in the drug culture who had totally cut himself off from involvement in society. In explaining why, this young man told Dr. Campbell he had spent "a whole summer" campaigning for political and social change and that nothing had come of it. "Therefore, I've had it. I quit. It's all hopeless," he concluded. Idealistic youth of every generation are vulnerable at this point. They expect too much too quickly, and all too often disillusionment becomes the child of illusion.

Actually, what Saul began took fifty years to complete. It was not until the time of Solomon that a centralized kingship was firmly established. Saul's efforts were the first step in a long and involved process. This is the way things almost always work. It is only in fairy tales that things are changed instantaneously; in the realm of reality, change usually comes slowly and in terms of a process. Had Saul recognized this, he might not have grown so disheartened. He might have seen that his efforts were the first steps in a long and involved process, that what he had done was not a failure but in fact a good beginning. How easy it is for any of us to have unrealistic expectations and thus distorted evaluations. Had Saul only realized that significant things take time, his whole life story might have had a different ending.

Saul's unrealistic expectations were, I believe, one reason for his eventual downfall, but there were other factors at work as well—like the lack of support Saul received from others, the imbalance of criticism and counsel. We have already emphasized that Saul came along at a particularly difficult moment in the history of Israel. The oppression of the Philistines had made the office of king a necessity, yet no one in Israel had any experience in this area or knew how to *be* a king. The old judge Samuel came nearer than anybody else to being an expert in national leadership, but he was at best half-hearted about this shift to kingship. And once Saul was anointed, Samuel did not really help him to find his way in this new frontier of leadership.

Is not this what so oftens happens in life? A person is given a difficult job by a group of people and then, instead of struggling with him and helping him find his way, the group sits back and lets him struggle alone until at last he "hangs himself." Then it is too late to salvage anything, and the group moves in to reject him. It seems to me this is what Samuel did to Saul. It could be that the misgivings Samuel had from the beginning got in his way. However, whatever the reason, he did not give Saul the kind of support the young king deserved. From the moment Saul was anointed king, all Samuel did was criticize and demean and reject the young man's efforts. It is little wonder that this one who did not ask for the job in the first place felt betrayed by the very one who had initiated the process.

There is a real lesson to be learned here as to how a collaborative process ought to work, be it in a relationship between parent and child, supervisor and trainee, or teacher and student. There must be more than negative criticism and abandonment if any progress is to be made. What the prophet Nathan did for David is so much better than what Samuel did for Saul. Nathan criticized David from time to time, but always at a point when something could still be done, and his criticism was always spoken with the hope of redemption. Samuel, on the other hand, waited until Saul had become totally mired in his own mistakes. Then the old judge came in with the word of total rejection and said, "You are finished, Saul. There is no hope for you." How could any struggling young man help but be demoralized by that kind of treatment? William Penn once said, "He has a right to censure who has a heart to help." One can only suspect that "the heart to help" was lacking in Samuel. The way he treated Saul suggests that part of him wanted the king to fail, and I feel strongly that this strategy of all negative criticism and no positive counsel contributed mightily to Saul's demise.

However, I doubt whether Samuel's lack of support could have had such an impact on Saul if it had not been for a third factor—Saul's self-image, how he viewed his place in the economy of God's purpose. For some reason, Saul was never able to accept himself—never able to feel, down to the bottom of his being, "By the grace of God I am what I am." He never saw himself as a gifted person, an instrument God had created for a specific task, and therefore was never able to take his place in the world—a place prepared for him before the foundations of the earth. I believe this inability—this identity problem—lies at the root of Saul's ultimate undoing. Samuel Miller has said quite perceptively that "our peace is in our place." But Saul was never able to experience such peace because he never seemingly accepted the gift of his place.

The first hint the biblical record gives us of this problem in Saul's life is his reaction to being approached by Samuel about being king. Saul was surprised and disclaimed any fitness for this kind of role; he even went and hid amid the baggage. Now such a response could be interpreted as commendable modesty, and it would have been appropriate if another human being had been trying to superimpose his will on Saul. But remember, this was something different; this was the call of God, the challenge of the One who had created Saul for this particular task. And this apparent modesty is really a clue to Saul's major flaw: he was never willing to believe that he had been created for this task and was capable of fulfilling it.

Saul's refusal to accept himself, which bred feelings of inadequacy and inferiority, steadily grew to alarming proportions. For example, it kept Saul from asserting himself when he had every right to do so. Once, on the eve of a battle with the Philistines, Saul waited almost a week for Samuel to come and offer the sacrifice that would consecrate the army before the battle. For reasons that are never explained, Samuel did not come when he promised, and as they waited the Israelites began to lose heart. Finally, when it appeared that Samuel was not going to appear, Saul made a sound decision. Rather than wait any longer and lose his advantage or go into battle unconsecrated, Saul ordered a lamb brought to him as God's leader and offered the sacrifice himself. But no sooner had he finished the ceremony than Samuel arrived and was incensed that Saul had preempted his priestly function. Saul ought to have backed Samuel down; after all, it was Samuel's tardiness, not Saul's arrogance, that had produced the crisis in the first place. But instead of standing his ground, Saul caved in completely before the defensive old man, and then let the whole situation demoralize him. Even when Saul was correct, he did not have the courage to recognize this fact and act on it. And such a failure of nerve is a sure sign of one who is not in touch with his own gift and therefore with his right to assert himself.

Saul's identity problem came to its ultimate expression in the feelings of envy that Saul developed for David in his later days. Elizabeth O'Conner has rightly noted that, whenever a person is envious of another, you can be sure that individual has never fully recognized and accepted his or her own gifts. If we are each in touch with our own uniqueness, then the gifts of others need not be threatening. I have my place, you have your place—all under the grace and providence of God. But if we are not secure at this point, then the abilities of others can make us anxious. This is obviously what happened to Saul. David first came to the king's attention as a shepherd lad who defeated the awesome Philistine giant, Goliath. He then joined the inner circle of Saul's household as an armor bearer and skilled musician and finally as a very effective military lieutenant. All through his life, David was never anything but an asset to Saul, but the older man could not recognize this fact. Saul became more and more insecure about David, until he finally became totally paranoid and turned on David completely. This mounting jealousy and hatred led to Saul's ultimate undoing, for it caused him to take his eyes off the real enemy—the Philistines—and to begin fighting an imaginary foe—David. Toward the end Saul seems to have gone completely insane, and finally provoked a battle he was sure to lose, falling on his own spear when defeat was imminent. He wound up figuratively "beside himself," a phrase which aptly describes the basic tragedy of Saul. This is where he chose to live his whole life—beside himself, that is, outside the place that God gave him. Saul's place was something he did not have to fight to keep; it was his by the gift of grace. Yet somehow Saul could never grasp this fact, and more than any other reason his failure to accept God's gift accounts for his unhappy demise.

In my judgment, there is no issue of any greater practical significance than this issue of self-image. How do you view the gift of God that is yourself? All depends on your response. To accept yourself positively and live creatively on the basis of what God has made you is the way to joy, but to deny and reject God's gift of yourself is the way to ruin.

I have heard it said that self-doubt and feelings of inferiority—in other words, low self-esteem—are at the root of all psychological illness. I'm inclined to agree. Until we come to terms with who God made us to be, we will always remain neurotic and unfulfilled. "Our peace is in our place," and our place is something God gives without our having to strive for it or earn it. This is the primal truth Saul could never accept.

Which brings me back to where we started. We have been looking at one of our spiritual ancestors, a man who came to his hour in history with a great sense of promise, but who in fewer than ten years was reduced to tragic failure. What went wrong? Most assuredly, the answer is a multiple thing. It could have been overexpectation or the lack of sympathetic support; these elements surely played a part. But at the bottom I am convinced that it was mostly this one thing—that Saul thought too little of himself. He was not willing to accept himself or act out of who he was by the grace of God. And this is why he ended up finally where he had always lived—"beside himself," outside the place that had been provided for him from the foundations of the earth.

4

WHO IS YOUR AUDIENCE?

Matthew 6:1–6, 16–18

I FIRST CAME ACROSS THE QUESTION that forms the title
of this chapter in a book by Keith Miller. In it, he described an insight into human nature he gained by observing his own reaction to reviews of his work. He
found that some decidedly negative reviews did not
bother him at all, because they were by people who really
did not matter to him, people whose reactions could be
explained by their ideological commitments. However,
there were certain other folks whose evaluations were a
different matter. Their words of approval warmed him,
and their criticism cut to the quick.

Miller concluded from all this that each one of us has a
select "audience" before whom we play the drama of our
lives. It may be only one person or a group of persons,
but what they think exerts enormous influence over our
daily actions. In fact, we entrust almost godlike power to
those we choose to be our "audience of significance."

While I had never heard the matter put in just these

terms, I sensed immediately the truth of Miller's insight. Life is in fact a stage, and each one of us is an actor "performing" to some kind of audience. We each feel the need for something outside ourselves to evaluate and authenticate our deeds.

Interestingly enough, this is an issue Jesus deals with in the Sermon on the Mount, especially the part contained in the sixth chapter of Matthew. When he says, "Beware of practicing your piety before men in order to be seen by them; for then you will have no reward from your Father who is in heaven" (Matt. 6:1, RSV), he is delving straight into this whole business of why we act as we do and whom it is we are trying to please as our "audience of significance." It appears to me that Jesus is doing two things in this verse and those that follow it.

First of all, he confronts us with the sobering fact that we *do* have an audience in all our living, and that it well may not be the one we naïvely assume it is. To illustrate this point, Jesus gives some daring examples indeed— the religious leaders of his day and the way they expressed their piety.

There were three great expressions of spiritual activity in ancient Judaism—almsgiving, prayer, and fasting— and since these were at the heart of religious practice, one would assume that they were to be done for God alone. "Notice, however," says Jesus, with his x-ray eyes, "for whom these acts are really performed." For example, almsgiving in that day had come to be accompanied by great fanfare. There were large, metal, trumpet-shaped coffers in the outer court of the Temple, and many Pharisees made a practice of getting their gifts broken down into the smallest form of currency. Then at the busiest time of the day, they would dump this hoard of coins into the coffer. Oh, the noise it would make and the attention it would attract! Or again, the pious Jews had the habit of praying regularly at nine, twelve, and three o'clock every day. Instead of praying at home or in the Temple or in some quiet place at those times, these religionists saw to it that they were on the busiest of street corners. There they would raise their hands and voices to heaven and stand out like pious jewels among the more careless masses. The practice of fasting was also dramatized to the hilt. Fasting had originally developed as a discipline toward some religious goal. When a person was anxious to achieve some particular objective, he would not even bother to eat; the practice of abstaining from food had therefore become the mark of intense commitment. However, certain Pharisees had allowed this means to an end to become an end in itself, and would go to great lengths to make sure everyone knew they were fasting.

With unerring insight, Jesus exposed this whole process for what it was—a series of religious acts played to other human beings, not to God. It must have been a startling revelation for these Pharisees to find out that the audience for all their religious activity was not at all the one they professed to have. Yet this is where Jesus starts with all of us in his ministry of truth—he confronts us with both the fact of and the identity of our "audience of significance."

As I observe what Jesus is doing at this point, I must admit I grow a bit uneasy, for what he detected in the lives of those Pharisees long ago is uncomfortably similar to what we do in our time and in our culture. If you should ask what is really important to most folk like us, the answer that stands out above all others is the opinion of our peers. When you talk about "audiences" and the significant people whose approval we covet, we middle-class Americans are blood kin to those Pharisees in Jesus' day in that our real "audience" tends to be our peer group—the people in our church or club or neighborhood or business. As we live out our lives, the question that haunts us at every turn is "What will *they* say? What will *they* think? How can I earn their approval and avoid their condemnation?"

Dr. Samuel Miller once observed with great wisdom that the realities of success and failure with one's peers have become in our day what salvation and damnation were in the Middle Ages. Back then, the thing a person feared most was displeasing God and "falling into the hands of an angry Deity." But today all of that is changed. We really do not give much thought to the ultimate dimension of our existence. Our hopes and fears are more immediate; they center on the opinions of our contemporaries. To most of us here, the most hideous of all possibilities would be to fail in the eyes of our friends and coworkers. To have a job and then lose it, or to own a fine house and be forced to sell it, or to have a child go a route that deviates from the accepted path of advancement—these are the terrors that haunt the souls of us modern folk. To have and go and do and be just like the other "people of distinction" is our substitute for heaven and salvation. This comes back to the first point Jesus was making: We have an audience to whom we play our lives and, for most of us, this audience is not God at all —not even in our religious actions—but a group of other human beings whose approval we crave at any cost.

Some churches have recognized this fact and proceeded to exploit it ruthlessly. I once knew of a fellowship that had a great reputation in material stewardship, and I was impressed until I got on the inside and found out how "the system" worked. I learned that one man in particular had unlimited brashness and gall. He was wealthy and prominent in the community and knew a lot about what went on financially, so he would go to church members and say threateningly, "I know what you have and what you ought to give. How would you like for so and so down the street to know you are not doing your part in the church? Certain facts have a way of getting around. Let me have a big pledge, or else." So help me, this was the kind of pressure that lay behind that impressive church budget, and those tactics could not have worked so effectively if the people in that church had not been pretty much like the Pharisees in Jesus' day—committed to an audience of peers and afraid above all to fail in their sight.

The first aspect of Christ's ministry in Matthew 6, then, is to establish the fact that each of us has an "audience of significance" and to expose its real identity. He makes us see that we are all influenced tremendously and decisively by whatever group we allow to be our audience, and he dares us to name that audience very specifically.

But he does not end the matter there—and that brings us to the second thing I believe Jesus is doing in this passage. As soon as we are made to realize who our audience *is*, Jesus goes on to show who our audience *ought to be*. He does this through the imagery of "rewards." This concept is admittedly confusing and difficult in the realm of religion, for many people understand rewards in terms of cheap bribes held out to influence behavior. I can certainly understand this kind of thinking, but I do not think this is what Jesus is talking about when he says the Pharisees have already received their "reward" and that the Father will "reward" those who do what Jesus says.

It is important to realize that rewards can come in two radically different forms. One kind of reward has nothing to do with the action it follows. It is a bribe—something superimposed and unrelated, like my offering my son a new car if he can make an "A" in calculus. However, there is another kind of reward that is organically tied to the action. In talking about this second kind of reward, I can say to my son, "If you make an 'A' in calculus and thus master this skill, you will be rewarded by having access to knowledge and possible job opportunities that come in no other way." This kind of reward involves the reality that, if we do such and such, certain consequences logically follow. After all, our actions do make a difference; they are seeds that produce a certain, predictable kind of harvest. And the promise of reward in this sense is not an artificial bribe but a realistic prediction of what one can expect from certain kinds of input.

It is reward in this latter, "organic" sense that Jesus has reference to when he speaks of someone's already "having their reward" or receiving it from the Father. What he means is this: If we make any person or group other than God our audience of significance, all we will get is that group and their limitations—what they are and what they will make us be. On the other hand, if we make Almighty God our audience, all the greatness of a living Father will be ours.

We have already noted that we are drastically affected by the audience we choose, and it should not be hard to see how the limits of such a group will become our limits as well. Let us say, for example, that I pick as an audience a certain peer group who think and dress and live and travel and entertain in a certain way. Their mores may not coincide exactly with the way I feel or with the certain unique qualities that are mine and mine alone. However, such a group has little toleration for individuality or purely personal tastes. To be approved one must conform and so my uniqueness is ground under, stifled, and crushed. What I am saying is that picking any audience except God always means bondage, limitation, the shackling of our true potential.

On the other hand, playing one's life to God as the ultimate point of reference is an altogether different matter, for according to Jesus God is our Father, our Maker, the One who knows better than anyone else what is in us and what ought to be brought out. He loves our uniqueness; it is his creation. He is not interested in blind conformity. The "reward" that comes from obeying this kind of God is that we become more and more of what we have in us to be. The wonder of the Christian gospel is summed up in this primal fact—God's will and our joy are synonymous. All he wants for us is that we become all he meant for us to be, and to enjoy this forever.

God, then, is the best possible audience we could have, the One to whom we ought to play in every moment of the day, if we knew what was good for us. But that is the problem—we do not yet believe that God is good. And so we enslave ourselves to those who limit us according to their images, rather than expand ourselves under the influence of him who made us and would enlarge us forever in his image.

It is right at this point that I understand the mission of Christ to earth, for he came "to show us the Father," to eradicate the false image we had of God as a demon or an indifferent manager or a tyrant. Jesus came to give a face to the mystery that is God, and on that face is the smile of a living Father. If this truth ever gets across to us, the answer to the question of who our audience is will fall in place. For, I repeat, if we know what is good for us, who would not prefer to play to a Father, and to be influenced by One who knows us best and loves us most, than to play to some group that will limit us according to their limits because they care so little about our uniqueness.

The secret of Jesus' life and joy and power lies right at this point: He knew God as his Father, and he played his whole life to him and him alone. "Thy will be done" was his most constant refrain. This is the meaning of salvation—to be free in God to become all that is in us to be. Why, then, settle for slavery? Why play to an audience that offers so little and takes so much?

I come back to the question that is an ultimate one: Who is your audience? I am indebted to Keith Miller for the form of the question, but to Jesus Christ for the pierc-

ing ministry that surrounds the issue. We all have an audience to whom we play our lives and by whom we are
tremendously affected. Who, then, will it be—our peers,
who can offer us only bondage and stifling limitation, or
the Father, who will lead us more and more to be all we
were meant to be? Inevitably, we will take on the image
of our audience. Whose image will it be—our peers on
earth, or our Father in heaven? *How wrong can this
man be I have no audience and never will
have one He is a lier when he say we all have
an audience I have no desire to please anyone but my God.*

5

FEAST OR FAMINE—
LIFE IS HOW YOU LOOK AT IT

Mark 14:22–25

YOU CAN OFTEN TELL a great deal about a person by observing how he or she eats. The act of taking in food is by no means a commonplace one; it is a process that is full of significance. This is true because, more often than not, the way we eat symbolizes the way we relate to life as a whole. The way I sit down to a table of food is usually reflective of how I sit down to the table of life. And the way I take in what is on the table will tell you a lot about how I go about incorporating all outside reality.

For instance, if I eat slowly and savor every morsel, you might conclude that I am sensitive to the beauty in the world around me and that I enjoy my entire life as much as I enjoy my food. On the other hand, if I bolt down my meal and rush to the door, you might guess that I live "in the fast lane," that I am impatient and always in a hurry for the next thing to happen.

Now of course we have to make allowances when we make these kinds of observations. If I pick at my food

51

and leave most of it on my plate, I may well be a person who is hard to please in other areas of life, but I may also be afraid of putting on weight or simply have a very small appetite. Similarly, a prodigious appetite may indicate a taste for excess, but it may also be a sign that I am accustomed to hard physical labor and need a lot of fuel.

Nonetheless, it is true that, whenever we sit down to eat, we have two options about the way we partake of what is put before us—and the choice we make from these two options says a lot about our attitude toward life in general. We can approach the meal with a negative spirit—wishing we were at a different table, critical of the way the food is cooked, unhappy about what we are being served. Or we can sit down with gratitude and appreciation that a meal has been provided for us, and enjoy what we have been given.

We have the same two options when we sit down at the table of life. We either can partake resentfully and bitterly of the events set before us, or we can respond positively and gratefully to these same realities. We humans are never free to determine what fare will be set before us, but we are free to decide how we will partake of it—whether in resentment or in gratitude. And there is a vast difference in which of these ways we choose to "eat."

An example of the former attitude can be found in the experience of the first human being. The second chapter of Genesis quaintly describes the process of God trying to provide for the many hungers of his newly made creature. First he is pictured as planting a garden so that Adam would have food to eat and shade in which to rest. Then he formed the rivers and seas to quench his thirst and gave him work to do so that there would be a sense of accomplishment in his existence. Finally he answered his need for companionship by creating first the animals and then another human being sufficiently like him that they could communicate but sufficiently different that they would be creative.

It is almost as if God were setting a banquet table before Adam and inviting him, "Take, eat, drink, participate fully." Yet how did Adam react to all this giftgiving? It soon became apparent that he was sullen and resentful and dissatisfied. He did not like his place at the table or the food set before him, nor did he trust the intentions of his Host. How do we know this? Because when the serpent began to cast aspersions on the whole arrangement, Adam fell for his story "hook, line, and sinker." Had Adam liked being human and been grateful for all the bounty laid before him, he would not have been vulnerable to the suggestion that he become something else or try a different diet. But he did not like being what he was, so he proceeded to grasp for the one thing in the Garden that had not been offered to him for food—fruit from "the Tree of the Knowledge of Good and Evil," the symbol of God himself.

Adam's kicking over his own table and making a beeline for the food on God's table was an act of rebellion and distrust, but note carefully that it was born of resentment. He did not like what he had been given and, according to Genesis, that is the reason human life has been in chaos ever since. And it is our ongoing refusal to accept the kinds of gifts God wants to give that continues to poison all of life and turn God's party of creation into a brawl. Here is one way of eating—the negative, resentful way—and look at the consequences that flow from it!

But we need now to set over against this image another way of eating—the example of the second Adam, Jesus of Nazareth. He came into the world as the first Adam did, but the attitude he assumed toward himself, toward God, and toward the events placed before him was distinctly different. Interestingly enough, whenever the Gospel writers depict Jesus as eating a meal, they describe him as doing what he would later do at the Last Supper: "[He] took bread, and blessed it. . . . he took the cup, and gave thanks."

This was more than just an ancient Jewish ritual; it is a picture of the way Jesus sat down to the banquet table of life, of how he related to what God was setting before him. Unlike the first Adam, Jesus did not despise his place in the order of things. He was not resentful of the fare that was placed before him. He did not mistrust the intentions of his Father. Rather, a grateful acceptance undergirded his whole life, and this opened the way to the joy and peace that so beautifully characterized him. Even on the last night of his life, at the supper table, he acted out the kind of reconciliation to God that he had come to effect in all persons. The way Jesus took the bread and blessed it and took the cup and gave thanks is a model of how life is to be lived at its deepest level.

I am convinced that here is the real secret of joyous and victorious living, and that it is within the grasp of every one of us. In terms of the events of life, we are not free to determine what will be set before us on the banquet table, but we are free to decide how we will partake of this fare. If we choose, we can relate negatively and resentfully to the things that happen to us and therefore turn all of life into agonizing conflict. Or, if we choose, we can follow the example of Jesus. We can learn to gratefully accept the things that happen to us and we can attempt to discover in each one the form of blessing that is assuredly there.

I had this truth graphically illustrated to me some years ago when I was making calls in the hospital. One afternoon I found an elderly member of my congregation in a state of utter misery. When I asked her how she was, she could do nothing but complain. She did not like the particular hospital she was in—the bed was too hard, the sheets too scratchy, and the staff not considerate enough.

When I noticed she was having to eat a soft diet, she began to lament that she had lost most of her teeth and could not chew well. On and on she went, cataloguing her complaints, and every time I tried to speak some positive word, she shot it down with her negativism.

I left that room thoroughly depressed, for I had never seen a human being more miserable. A few minutes later, I entered the room of another woman who was also up in years and facing a painful situation. Because the other visit was fresh in my mind, I immediately began to commiserate with this woman about her lot. And yet, from the first, her attitude was noticeably different. When I suggested that having to be in the hospital was an unpleasant experience, she countered by saying she was very grateful that there were such places when one was as sick as she was. I surmised that the noise of the hospital and the hardness of the bed made hospital life inferior to life at home, but she said, "No, this bed suits me just fine, and I actually enjoy the company of the nurses coming in and out." I saw that she too was on a soft diet, and I remarked that she must find this difficult, but a smile came to her face as she said, "Well, I just have two teeth left, but, thank the Lord, they hit!"

Here was a person up against the same set of circumstances as the woman I had visited earlier, yet this one had chosen to be grateful for what she had rather than resentful for what she did not have! There was no anger or resentment or discontent in her. Somehow she had accepted her place at the table and the particular fare that was being set before her at that time.

As I walked out of that room, I realized anew what a difference our attitude can make in our lives. From an outward standpoint, these two women were being served the same thing, but for one it was garbage, for the other a banquet and the difference lay in their attitude—in how they chose to eat. The second woman had learned the secret of what Jesus did on the last night of his life; she was taking the bread and blessing it, taking the cup and giving thanks. In this way, she was proving to be more than a conqueror of the difficult events that she was facing.

The question then really is: How do you eat? It is a significant inquiry for it pertains to how you relate to the events that cascade in upon you day by day. Do you regard them resentfully and live in an atmosphere of discontent? Or do you relate to them gratefully and thus find a way to live through your difficulties? Jesus took the bread and blessed it. He took the cup and gave thanks. And therein lies the secret, open to all who will learn it. The reconciliation to God which Jesus came to bring about consists of sitting down to the table of life with a thankful heart. And what better time is there to begin than right now?

6

EXILES IN TIME

Psalm 137; Hebrews 3:7–14

ONE OF THE MOST EXCITING THINGS that has happened to me in a long time was a conversation I had recently with a man named Sam Keen. I must acknowledge that I am using the word *conversation* in a different way than is usual, for the two of us did not sit down face-to-face as we have done in the past; rather, we conversed by means of a part of a book he had written. But this was the kind of book that so "turned me on" that every few paragraphs I would find myself putting it down and talking back to it, reflecting on the many implications it raised. It was also the kind of book that set me in dialogue with many other sources—the Bible, my family, and several other people with whom I had contact.

All in all, my "conversation" with Sam Keen was a thrilling, life-giving experience for me. And, as is often the case, when I have received life, my first desire is to pass it on to others. This, then, is what I shall attempt in this chapter. Freely have I received from a wonderful experience; freely now I shall try to give that you might receive as well.

The title of the conversation that took place between Sam Keen and myself was "Exile and Homecoming," but the real issue was the question of time and how one can live gracefully with the powers of past, present, and future. Keen began by describing the plight of the exile, and by suggesting that this is where most of us are when it comes to our lives; that is, we find ourselves separated from our homeland, from that place in time where we would most like to be.

One of the forms this spirit of exile takes is "nostalgia," which is a longing to go back in time, to return to a condition that seems, from the perspective of the present, to be ideal or just about perfect. The word *nostalgia* itself is a Greek derivative that means "to return home." It is the melancholy that accompanies wanting to get back to one's origins. We have a classic illustration of this feeling-state in Psalm 137. Here were Jewish exiles ripped away from their beloved homeland and filled with hatred for where they were. To remember Zion, to get back to the way it once had been—this was the ultimate passion of those who wrote this psalm.

The other form the spirit of exile takes is the urge to revolution, which is as absolute in its feeling about the future as nostalgia is about the past. Here is the desire to change everything by embracing the vision of the "Great Not Yet," to tear down what is and start some sort of utopia. This attitude, too, can be found in the Bible, in that strand of literature known as "apocalyptic." Books like Daniel and the Book of Revelation predict the overthrow of the present and look forward to the day when a brand new heaven and earth will descend out of the sky straight from God.

The feeling of being exiles in time, then, is very common to our human situation, and can be seen not only in the biblical material but in our own times as well. Stop and think about it for a moment—is not part of the reason for so much turbulence in our country right now the fact that nobody much likes the present, and that some people are trying to move out of it in a backward direction while others are trying to flee forward? No wonder there is such confusion! We are like a theater full of people in which someone cries "Fire." The basic reaction is the same—to get out of that place—but as some people head for the back door and others head for the front door, they crash headlong into each other and run the danger of trampling each other to death in their efforts to escape.

So it is, I think, with all of us exiles in the last years of the twentieth century. Some people today are obsessed with the memory of "the good old days," "a return to prosperity," and the "virtues that made this country great," and they seem intent on getting back there even if they repress everyone in the process. Others (less visible now than a few decades ago, but by no means out of sight) are just as sure that everything old is utterly worthless, and that we must level our whole nation by revolution before we can begin to build the better world of tomorrow. These two groups could not be more different in what they are running toward, and yet they are just alike in what they are running from—the here and now, the present, the actualities of this moment in history.

Sam Keen is right, I feel, in saying that most of us are exiles, one way or the other. Your way may be the nostalgic form of exile that longs for a golden age that existed somewhere back yonder in "once upon a time," or it could be the revolution form of exile that looks ahead to some "alabaster city" or utopia. Either way, however, to long for a time other than this one, be it past or future, is to be an exile. And if we are honest, does that not include most of us? Our bodies may be present in the here and now, but our hearts? They are in exile. And our feet? They are running either backwards in nostalgia or forward toward revolution as fast as they can.

This was one of the places where I had to put down the book and reflect long and deeply on the image of exile. What an accurate mirror this is of the confusion of our time! Yet eventually I picked up the book again, for alongside the condition of exileship was the event called "homecoming," which is obviously the solution to this problem of separation.

Sam Keen began describing this reality by acknowledging his own involvement in both forms of exile. He spoke of having "wasted his substance," like the Prodigal Son of Jesus' parable, in the far country of both past and future. For example, he had been raised in an intensely religious home in Maryville, Tennessee, and had first sought to find his identity in the past by imitating the great hero figures of the Bible like David and Moses and Paul. (I think this is a very common reaction of impressionable, idealistic youth.) Then he had grown older, and the remoteness of these hero figures to the peculiarities of his own time had grown greater and greater, until by the time he was a student at Harvard University he was finding it impossible to cope with life solely by imitating stylized figures out of the past.

I know exactly the frustration he was experiencing, for the very form that history assumes tends to oversimplify life and to make it seem as if complicated processes were really quite easy for our ancestors. For example, I grew up thinking of Abraham Lincoln as the Great Emancipator, as one who was born in a log cabin and then shot like a rocket to a place of power, where he immediately set about abolishing slavery and setting a whole race of people free. Then a few years ago on vacation I decided to read Carl Sandburg's detailed biography of Lincoln, and I discovered that Lincoln had been very much a moderate on the slavery question. He had made many speeches advocating slavery and had spoken negatively about the Black person's natural capabilities. His real concern in the 1860s had been to preserve the Union and to unite this country, not to be the champion of the abolition movement.

Reading Sandburg's biography of Lincoln shattered my generalized images and made me realize how easily memory can shade over into mythology. As the immediacy of an experience recedes, we tend to recall only the central theme—the residue, so to speak—and all the ambiguity and uncertainty which surrounded it fades away. This is why every attempt to find an exact model to imitate out of the past will always produce frustration, for we can never really know what pressures and alternatives our heroes had to face. History seldom records just how complicated significant decision making really is. The Old Testament accounts of Moses, for instance, are really summaries of what the man was able to do and, like all history, they make life appear easier than it was for him as he lived it and than it will be for us as we live it. That is why heroes out of the past can guide us or inspire us, but they can never be exact models. They can never take off our hands the responsibility of deciding for ourselves what we must do. No matter how appealing it is, nostalgia cannot furnish us our individual identities.

However, the future is just as unsatisfactory as the past in this regard. Keen relates how in college he shifted from one extreme to follow the other. He decided to follow the advice that one needs to set goals out ahead and to work in order to reach them, for such projections are what redeem the present of its emptiness and boredom. So he did this; he focused on the goal of getting a Ph.D. and becoming a professor, and in good American fashion proceeded to postpone all present satisfactions in the name of reaching that goal. He speaks of failing to cultivate the soil of his own experience, of becoming "an intellectual sharecropper on the fields of absentee landlords" such as Plato, Hegel, and all the rest. It was one form of an experience so familiar to us all—projecting our joys and hopes into the future and saying, "As soon as I get the mortgage paid (or the children are grown or I get out of school), I will do this and that and satisfaction will be mine."

Well, Keen eventually got his degree and began to be called "Doctor" and was hired as a professor, but he found that the magic he had hoped for did not descend. All that "milk and honey" he had anticipated during those years of deferred satisfaction did not begin to flow. Rather, having reached "the promised land" after all these years, he found it bleak and disappointing. Having put all his eggs in this one future basket, he found them unhatched and empty.

Keen writes movingly of how the waves of disillusionment washed over him. He had looked for meaning and dignity in both past and future, only to be betrayed, and he found himself crying out in desperation, "What can I do that will give dignity and meaning to my life?"—a cry using different words but of the same substance as the biblical cry, "What must I do to be saved?"

And then one night in a Manhattan hotel room, Keen awoke with the answer dancing up and down before his mind. It was: "Nothing, nothing at all." What finally broke through his feverish anguish was the realization that all along he had been obsessed by the wrong question. At bottom there was really nothing he could *do* to give meaning and dignity to his life, for these are not things that can be earned; they are given and received out of God's grace. Dignity and meaningfulness either come with the territory, he thought, or they do not come at all. Worthiness is not contingent on human effort; it is given with our being. It is not the result of works, of which we can boast, but the gift of grace—pure and sheer and utterly outright. There in the night it suddenly came over my friend Sam Keen that he had been "riding on an ox, looking for an ox," and that what he had sought so earnestly in both the past and future had been right with him all the time—the present—and he had not known it.

This was the moment of "homecoming," of being delivered from the exile of nostalgia and revolution, of being given all over again the gift of himself—the gift of the here and now, the gift of present actualities rather than myths and fantasies. It was a moment much like the moment when the Prodigal "came to himself" and decided it was all right just to be the son that he was in the home where he had been born. It was an experience like that of Russell Conwell's famous man who searched the world over for diamonds, only to find acres of them in his own backyard. It was exactly what Paul and Augustine and Luther had experienced and expressed in the doctrine of "justification by faith." They all learned, in one form or another, that human salvation is not dependent on human action, but is a free gift of God, and that being has priority over doing when it comes to a person's worth.

And here was another place where the book had to be laid down, for what had happened to Sam Keen had happened to me not too long ago, when it had really hit me emotionally that I was worth something *because of God* and not because of my efforts. The authoritative word of God to me was the verse, "You are the light of the world" (Matt. 3:14). It does not say, "Earn light," or "Become light," or "Out-achieve others and you will be paid off in light." It says, rather, "You are light. This is the gift of creation. Your worth is already in you because God has placed it there. Therefore, let your light shine. Give away the gifts that have been given you, that men may see the good thing God has made you to be and glorify him who is in heaven."

This was the moment of my own "homecoming" from

the exile of competitiveness, in which I had striven so hard to make something of myself by "coming out the number-one man." And I am convinced this is at the heart of biblical salvation and wholeness—the moment when we are given the freedom and power to participate in God's affirmation of who we are and of who all persons are made to be. Such a homecoming to one's self also means coming home to the present, to the here and now, and not needing to run into exile any more. It frees us to live in time as we were really meant to live—in the here and now.

That does not mean, however, that we are to live as if the past and future did not exist. One of the things I like most about Sam Keen's analysis is that Keen does not isolate the present from its roots and its destiny as do so many others today. In trying to correct the distortions of both nostalgia and revolution, some writers would either have us live without memory or without anticipation, and this is both inhuman and impossible. To be a human being alive in history means always to begin in the middle of something, with a world that was here long before we were, and with human nature that was already in motion years before we awakened into consciousness. Similarly, being human means being a creature that can plan and hope. There is a place for projecting into the future and taking responsibility for extending the kind of joy we want into the days ahead. What is needed is not nostalgia or revolution but a model of life that is firmly planted in the present but that also resonates openly with both past and future.

This brings us back to the idea of homecoming. Homecoming, as Sam Keen so movingly revealed to me, and as I would like to share with you, is a matter of changed perspective more than a change of location or even nature. This is true in terms of temporality—in coming to accept where we are in time. But it is also true in a deeper sense. Homecoming means realizing to the depths of one's being that "by the grace of God, I am what I am," and accepting this and embracing this and learning to love this. For it is the gift of God that he accepts us and affirms us as we are, in the here and now, and that he waits to welcome us with open arms when we return from our "far countries" of exile.

7

GOING THROUGH HOME

Mark 3:19–21, 31–35;
John 19:25–27

THERE IS SOMETHING about the Thanksgiving season that causes us to think about "home"—that is, to look back on where we come from and to think about the events of the past. Each year at this time our nation does this; we recall the familiar images of our Pilgrim forefathers and all those events that make up our national heritage. I submit to you that such a periodic taking stock of the past is a healthy discipline indeed, both for nations in a corporate sense and for individuals in a personal sense, because, as we saw in the previous chapter, there is no way fully to understand what we are at a given moment apart from what has happened in the moments and days and years that have come before. We all have our personal histories that reach back further than memory and deeper than consciousness. And, although we actually do our living in the here and now, the dimension of pastness is a powerful factor in the composition of our lives.

For this reason, if we want to come to terms authentically with the realities of who we are and where we are going, we all need to ask ourselves questions like: How do I live with that part of the past that lives in me? How am I relating to all that has gone on before this moment? Are the events of my past serving as building blocks for a better future or stumbling blocks that keep me from growing? Is the past a force to lift me up or hold me down? These are the issues I want us to explore in this chapter.

Now, the moment we turn our eyes behind us and attempt to get in touch with our own history, we find ourselves confronting a vast complexity. No person's past is a simple, one-quality sort of thing. No matter who you are, there is bound to be both light and darkness, good and evil, beauty and horror in the way you have traveled up to this moment. The things you have done and the things that have been done to you intertwine to produce a varied mixture. For all of us the past is a blend of light and darkness, hurt and blessing, and this is what we have to face as we seek to come to terms with this dimension of our existence.

When we take stock of the past, the temptation is always to oversimplify, to concentrate on only part of our heritage. This can take the form of looking solely at the darkness of the past and becoming obsessed either with our own guilt or with all the hurts and neglects and cruelties that have been inflicted on us by others. This kind of morbid preoccupation with the darkness of the past can lead to disastrous personal results.

However, the same mistake can be made in the other direction as well; we can concentrate only on the light in our past and deny that there was any darkness. This leads to the distortion of perception called "nostalgia," which, as we pointed out in the previous chapter, is the yearning for an idealized and oversentimentalized past. Nostalgia longs to return to "the good old days." But trying to do so, of course, leads to pathetic disillusionment, for no one—no matter how deep the desire—can swim back up the stream of time. The often-quoted words of Thomas Wolfe are still true: "You can't go home again."

The fact is that neither one of these extremes is a healthy way of dealing with the experiences of the past. To look exclusively at either the good or the bad is to have partial vision. We must come to terms with the fact that both of these dimensions exist and we must accept them accordingly. This is where the spirit of the Thanksgiving season can be of practical help to us. Thanksgiving involves looking back, as I have said, but with a sense of reality and gratitude; it means looking at *all* that is behind. When this is done faithfully, the way becomes clear for us to make creative rather than destructive use of the past.

This idea was set forth very powerfully some time ago by Carlyle Marney. At the time he was addressing himself to the issue of finding one's identity and confronting—as he put it—the "self-soul." He acknowledged the need to face up to the darkness of one's being and one's past—"those awful, primal, prowling powers that push little Id to make me serve the self." Yet Marney did not stop with such grim introspection. He suggested that if this is all one does, one may well drown in the dirty waters of self-despising. What is needed alongside an awareness of Original Sin, he said, is "an awareness of an Original Love."

What he meant by this was that, from the very beginning and down to the deepest level of our beings, we have been loved and cared for throughout our lives. At the very moment of our birth, when we were naked and bloody and of little beauty or worth, someone picked us up, washed us, cared for us, and loved us. This act is a symbol of the countless ways goodness has come to us from family and friends and from God himself. For all the slights and hurts and cruelties each one of us has had to endure, goodness and mercy have also followed us all the days of our lives. To recognize this fact is to be grateful—and this is the right place to begin in a healthy handling of the past. It is precisely this awareness of light and goodness interwined through all the ugliness of our past that enables us to gain a sense of strength.

Marney's words at this point are moving and beautiful indeed: "From here [that is, the dawn of gratitude], a man can begin to make peace with the culture that spawned him; with the parents that shaped and misshaped him; with the institutions that blessed and provincialized and distorted him. From here he can make peace. *He can go through home again.* He can accept the stuff that God had at His disposal for making him."

In my judgment, the phrase, "going through home again" describes real maturity when it comes to dealing with the past. To want only to go home again and stay there would be as wrong as it is impossible, for this implies a sentimentalizing of the past and a refusal to face up to its darkness and its faults. The desire to return to the past the way one would return to the womb is not a healthy one.

By the same token, to want to leave home altogether and have nothing whatsoever to do with the roots of our being or the sources which spawned us is just as unhealthy a desire. However much hurt and darkness may have been in the past, there was also light and love in some measure if we will only acknowledge it. To deny the past, to want never to go home again, is to cut oneself off from a vital aspect of life, a dimension of rich perspective. A person without a memory is only half a person; amnesia is a handicap, not a blessing.

It is far better, in my judgment, to do what Marney says here—"to go through home again." This phrase balances beautifully both the light and darkness of the past and enables us to accept what can be accepted out of the past and to reject what must be rejected. This is the way to authentic selfhood, and gratitude is the perspective that emboldens us to risk this process of coming to terms with the past. We would hardly have the courage to press on if we felt that the past were nothing but darkness. It is the realization that light has been there all the while, running all the way back, that gives us the strength to keep coping with life. And being aware of light is simply another way of describing gratitude. When I am willing to take the time to move back through my days—in short, to "count [my] blessings, name them one by one"—then it will surprise me to realize "what the Lord hath done." The awareness that "goodness and mercy have followed me all the days of my life" counteracts the acids of bitterness and gives me a positive perspective on the unfolding of my life.

Life, then, is not solely a process of going back home again or of moving away from home completely, but of going through home again and making use of both its darkness and its light. And gratitude is what enables us to deal with the past, to take what has happened and to learn from it—to use it to climb creatively rather than being immobilized by bitterness and guilt.

It is clear to me that this is the way Jesus lived his life. He was born into a home of loving yet imperfect people, just as most of us are. There was obviously some darkness in those early days (Mary and Joseph did not always understand what was unfolding in this unique child of promise, and at times—such as in the incident at the Temple in Jerusalem—they were harsh and unfeeling toward him. The instincts to dominate and control were very real factors here, as they are in most homes. In fact, even after Jesus was a grown man and well into his ministry, both his mother and his brothers became upset with what he was doing and attempted to come seize him and take him home by force. For this reason we never see

Jesus being sentimental about the past. There in Capernaum he resisted the attempts of his family to get him to go back home again. There was no nostalgia in him that remembered only the light and thus longed to swim back up the stream of time to some imagined "good old days."

But this did not mean Jesus was bitter about his past. He did not reject it or try to turn away from it completely, but rather manifested a deep appreciation for the love and support that had been given to him from the beginning. In fact, one of his last acts on the cross demonstrated his attitude toward the past; he spoke to his disciple John and asked him to care for his mother in her old age. After all, she had cared for him in his time of helplessness, and he did not want her neglected when her time of need arrived. In other words, Jesus was grateful for the way he had come into history and for the human sources—imperfect as they were—that God had used to bring him into the world and to nurture him. For him the past became the foundation of the future—something positive and not negative, a set of building blocks rather than stumbling blocks. And this is what the past can become for each of us, if we will let it, by the exercise of gratitude. We have all been blessed as well as hurt by the events of the past. Gratitude provides the perspective by which we can use our past experiences creatively rather than being destroyed by them.

8

WHAT JESUS BELIEVES
ABOUT YOU

Matthew 4:1–11

FROM TIME TO TIME, in church or elsewhere, you have probably been asked what you believe about Jesus, and this is an exceedingly important question. In this chapter, however, I want to turn the issue around and ask, "What does Jesus believe about you?"

My concern here is the view of human nature that caused Jesus to act as he did. I sometimes hear people say that *what* a person believes is not important as long as he or she is sincere, but I think that is utter nonsense! Belief and action are not two separate entities; they are part and parcel of the same process. We act as we do because of what we believe; those depth images called "beliefs" are the foundations of all behavior. This was true for Jesus as well as for the rest of us. Back of the particular way Jesus related to people was a certain vision of human nature—what we are and what we can become. This is what I want us to focus on now. What does Jesus believe about you, about me, about all creatures called human beings? It is a crucial question indeed.

I must admit that my insight at this point has been greatly sharpened by one of the world's great novels, Feoder Dostoevsky's *The Brothers Karamazov*. A famous section of this novel—a fantasy related by one of the characters—is called "The Grand Inquisitor." This famous piece of fiction directly addresses the issue of what Jesus believes about human beings. With probing insight, it calls Jesus' whole approach into question and, in so doing, raises the issues that must be faced at this point.

"The Grand Inquisitor" is set in sixteenth-century Spain, at a time when the authority of the Roman Church was at its height and heretics were being burned daily "to the glory of God." In the square before the Cathedral in Seville, Jesus appears again in bodily form. While he does not say anything, the people immediately recognize him, for the same loving compassion that warmed and excited the people of Galilee streams forth once again from his person; men and women are attracted to him as to a giant magnet. The power of such love is innately healing, and before long a blind man has recovered his sight and a seven-year-old girl has been raised back to life.

A near frenzy of excitement is beginning to build there in the cathedral square when the aged Cardinal of Seville, the Chief Inquisitor, happens to come by. He is ninety years old, full of worldly wisdom and hardened by decades of exercising absolute authority. He sees immediately what is occurring and who has reappeared. However, instead of falling on his knees at the sight of the Lord, he quickly orders the guards to arrest Jesus and put him in prison, and the people fall back submissively as they are accustomed to do. That night, all alone, the Inquisitor pays a visit to Jesus and proceeds to tell him in what ways he was mistaken in his ministry.

The Grand Inquisitor begins by asking, "Why have you come back to hinder us?" And then he says, in essence, "You were wrong, Jesus—totally, absolutely wrong in your assessment of human nature. You related 'up' to human beings, as if they were really children of God and thus capable of deciding things for themselves, of taking responsibility for their lives and for the world. You treated them as if they were partners with God, when in fact they are by nature nothing but slaves and children— weak, unstable, rebellious.

"What you failed to understand, Jesus, is that human beings cannot be free and happy at the same time. For one thing, they are not *good* enough to handle freedom. There is a corruption in them that rises to the surface as soon as the controls are taken off. Only anarchy and destruction result when humans are allowed to be free. Nothing is more insupportable either for individuals or society than this thing you valued so—freedom. Human beings aren't strong enough to handle this power! They really do not want the burden of having to decide things for themselves. They have no greater desire than finding someone to whom they can turn over this cursed gift of freedom. You really did not love human beings, Jesus, for you expected too much of them.

"Where you made your mistake was at the beginning of your ministry in the wilderness. The Spirit of this world came to you there and tried to show you what would work, but you would not listen to him. Don't you remember how he said, 'Humans have three needs and three only—the need to be fed, the need to be mystified, the need to be dominated'? He tried to get you to turn stones into bread, for then you could have made people happy. There is no crime, there is no sin, only hunger! Humans are little more than mouths and stomachs. That wise Spirit also tried to get you to jump off the pinnacle of the Temple and dazzle the people. They want to be mystified, to be made to feel that understanding things is beyond them and that thus it is all right for them to accept blindly whatever is done to them. He also tried to get you to put on the mantle of Caesar up there on the mountain, for humans want to be ruled, to be dominated, to be told what to do.

"The Spirit of this world understood human nature, but you would not listen to him. You with your impossible dreams of sonship and freedom and responsibility. I can hear you now: 'Man does not live by bread alone. They are more than mouths.' You refused to dazzle their senses or stupify them with the miraculous, because you believed they could think for themselves. And you would not take the role of Caesar and get involved in the only process that works in this world—the process of power, coercion, domination. You held out that human beings are more than pawns and deserve better treatment.

"Well, hear this, foolish Dreamer: We have accepted the gifts that you rejected there on the mountain, and we are now proceeding to correct your work. We love people realistically and are willing to treat them as the slaves they are. We are not about to let you come again and revive your erroneous ways. We will someday conquer the earth and rule humankind as they must be ruled. You were wrong, Jesus—totally and absolutely wrong about people—and unless you leave on your own right now, we will kill you all over again."

I trust you can see now why I am so impressed with this vignette. Here the basic issues of human nature are raised profoundly and cogently. What about Jesus' understanding of what we are? Was he right or wrong in relating "up" instead of "down" to us?

Obviously, there is considerable evidence at hand to confirm the Inquisitor's low view of human nature. For example, *are* humans good enough to handle freedom responsibly? In discussing the first temptation posed to Jesus by the Spirit of this world, the Grand Inquisitor asserted that as long as people are free there will never be bread enough to feed everyone. No matter how much

production is increased, he said, it will never be suffi-
cient, for people are inherently so insecure and selfish
that the "haves" will continue to hoard the surplus rather
than to share it with the "have nots." The only way for all
humans to be fed is for every human to be enslaved.

Now I wish I could stand up in the face of this charge
and say to the Inquisitor, "You are wrong about human
nature. We are better than that." Yet look around just
now at what is happening in this country. We are fast approaching a trillion-dollar gross national product—far
higher than any nation has ever achieved. However, instead of this enabling everyone to have at least enough,
all signs point to the fact that the gap between the
"haves" and the "have nots" is growing wider, and that
children are still starving in America. Or to put the issue
on a personal level, ask yourself this question: If somehow in 1983 my income would suddenly be tripled, honestly now, what would I do with the increase? How
much of it would find its way to the people who do not
yet even have enough for the necessities of life, and how
much of it would go to increasing my own list of
luxuries? How many more hungry children would be fed,
or how many additional color televisions would be
bought? The point is, if left free, how responsible are we
for the needs of the whole human family? Was the Inquisitor right that we are so insecure and selfish by nature that we cannot be trusted with freedom? Will there
ever be bread enough for all if we remain free, or does
some form of totalitarianism offer the only hope for fair
distribution of resources? I must confess that I find pondering such a question deeply disturbing.

And what about that other charge—that we are not
strong enough to handle freedom, yea, that we do not
even want to bother with its burden? This is the facet of
the subject that took me a long time to recognize. I grew
up assuming that everyone wanted to be free and that,

the problem was one of tyranny—that is, power-mad figures like Hitler or Stalin who were always trying to take
freedom away from people. However, I have come to
realize that tyranny is only one aspect of the problem.
The other side is the fact that often people *do* seem to prefer the security of being ruled to the responsibility of rul-
ing themselves.

Eric Fromm was a young Jewish psychiatrist in Berlin
in the 1920s and '30s, and he watched with amazement as
Hitler rose to power. Fromm wrote later that the Führer
did not have to conquer the Germans by force. They were
so divided and dispirited that they literally handed over
their hard-won freedoms and said, in essence, "Please,
take over our lives, our country, our fortunes. We want
security more than independence. The burden of freedom is too heavy." This has happened more than once in
history, and that, of course, is exactly what the Inquisitor
was claiming—that human beings are slaves at heart, too
weak and fearful to assume the responsibility for our own
lives or for the world.

There is much in the human scene, then, to suggest
that the Inquisitor was right in his low estimate of human
nature. But is that the total story? I do not think so! There
is much to be said on the other side of the question, the
Grand Inquisitor notwithstanding. I believe the Gospel of
John was correct in saying that Jesus did not have to be
told about human nature, for he knew what was humankind (2:25). Let us look at that issue more closely.

What the Tempter tried to get Jesus to do in the wilderness was to accept a low view of human potential and
thus relate "down" to humankind. But Jesus countered
this with the vision of human personhood inherent in the
Old Testament. He had been steeped from his childhood
in images like those in the eighth Psalm, which declares
that human beings were created "little less than God,"
crowned "with glory and honor," and "given . . . domi-

nation over the works of [God's] hands." Not slaves, but sons—not children, but colaborers with God—this is what Jesus believed human beings to be, and this is why he chose to relate "up" to them rather than "down," to concentrate on their high potential rather than settling for the lowest common denominator. And what resulted from Jesus' efforts? What came of appealing to the best instead of the worst in the human race?

The Book of Acts gives a convincing answer to this question. Look, for example, at the experience of Simon Peter. When Jesus first met him, he was the kind of weak, childlike creature the Inquisitor talks about. But how did Jesus relate to him? According to John's Gospel, the very first thing he said was: "You are a rock." That is, "I see in you the potential to become a strong and courageous and fearless leader." And the point is, Peter became this! The man you see walking the pages of the Book of Acts is not a childish slave looking for someone to feed him and mystify him and dominate him. Rather, he is depicted as standing up to rulers and mobs and pressure the way a strong son of God would stand. Now, to be sure, Peter did not become like this overnight, but he did eventually realize his potential because Jesus related "up" to his heights rather than "down" to his depths.

Jesus' way of relating had the same impact on countless others. The early Christians became not only strong enough to handle freedom, but good enough as well. By that I mean that there was a time when human beings were free and there was bread enough for everyone. It was said of the first century church that "no one was in need." By appealing to the highest instincts of the early Christians, Jesus did motivate them to share and to be concerned "one for the other." This has happened again and again in Christian history. Totalitarianism is not the only solution to the "bread" problem. There is in human nature the capacity to share and even to sacrifice for others, and this is the part of us Jesus attempts to enhance.

I repeat, therefore, the Book of Acts is glowing evidence of what the faith of Jesus in action can produce. As many as believed him—that is, had faith in his faith in them—"to them gave he power to become the sons of God" (John 1:12, KJV). Jesus' willingness to relate "up" to human beings paid off.

There is a basic reason for this—a process called "self-fulfilling prophecies." Let's face it; what we expect to happen affects how we act, and this in turn affects what actually does happen. One of the flaws in the Grand Inquisitor's case was that he failed to recognize the potency of belief in shaping what human beings become. In looking on men and women as slaves and as children, and in relating to them as such, he was actually helping to make and keep them that way.

Now, if I had decided when my son was five that he had reached his full potential, and if I had begun to relate to him accordingly, my very actions would have shaped him in that direction. Expectations are exceedingly formative, both positively and negatively—a fact which the Inquisitor overlooked. He mistook the beginning for the end; that is, he saw human beings as they start out in childhood—when they are weak and dependent and unsure—and concluded that this was all there was to them. But Jesus really knew what was in humankind—the potential as well as the actual—and in relating "up" to us he was both closer to the human reality and instrumental in evoking its full potential.

I like the story of the sculptor who worked for several months on a likeness of Abraham Lincoln. Every night a cleaning lady swept up the chips and watched the slow unfolding of the project. When the statue was finished, she complimented the work and then asked earnestly,

"But tell me, how did you know that Mr. Lincoln was in that rock?"

This is a good illustration of how Jesus related to men and women. He looked at rock-like people—rough, unseemly, shapeless—and saw inside the makings of magnificent human beings. Jesus had this kind of faith in human nature—that while we might be childish and slavelike in our present condition, we do not have to remain that way. We can be children of the Most High, responsible colaborers with him. This is why Jesus said no to the temptation to relate "down" to us, why he chose to relate "up" to our best, our "might be," our Mr.-Lincoln-in-the-rock. And I am willing to stake my life and my ministry on the belief that Jesus, not the Grand Inquisitor, was right!

9

THE PRESUMPTION OF DESPAIR

John 11:15–16; 20:24–29

SEVERAL YEARS AGO I came across the phrase, "the mystery that is every man." From the moment I saw it I liked it, because it reminds me of a fact about every person who has ever lived—that everyone is a dynamic, mysterious reality, always growing and changing and for that reason never completely or totally known. Every time I have concluded I knew all about another person, I have been proven mistaken by the disclosure of a facet I never dreamed existed. For this reason, relationships with other people need to remain radically open-ended if we are to understand them rightly.

This has certainly been my experience with that disciple of our Lord's named Thomas. He is by no means one of the pivotal figures of the New Testament. The fact that his name appears midway down the list of disciples in all the synoptic Gospels implies that he was neither the greatest nor the least of the twelve. He is mentioned specifically only in John's Gospel. For some time, however, this disciple has intrigued me, and as I have sought to get better acquainted with him across the centuries, my understanding of him has changed considerably, going through several stages.

At the beginning, I thought of Thomas solely in terms of his stereotype—as the doubter, the one who refused to believe that Jesus had been raised from the dead until he saw the evidence for himself. Perhaps, because I tend to be a doubter myself, I was attracted to him for that very reason! Later on, however, I came to see that this image—like all stereotypes—did not do justice to the man. The late Dr. J. B. Weatherspoon spurred me on at this point, for once I heard him preach a sermon in which he "took up for Thomas" and pointed to several positive characteristics that are usually overlooked.

For example, in John 11, when Jesus stated his intention to go and see about Lazarus, who had died in Bethany near Jerusalem, all the disciples counseled him against it. The last time they had been in Judea the authorities had become very hostile to Jesus, and to go back just then seemed risky business indeed. But Jesus had already "set his face toward Jerusalem" and was intent on going, and it was Thomas who spoke up and said, "Let's go with him, danger and all." Revealed here was a capacity of loyal friendship. Thomas was no fair-weather acquaintance; once committed to a friend, he was the kind to stick with him through thick and thin.

Thomas also had the endearing trait of radical honesty. In John 14, Jesus was expounding to the disciples about going to the Father, and wound up by saying, "The way I am going you know"—to which Thomas replied, "No, Jesus, we do not know where you are going; how can we know the way?" Here was the willingness to acknowledge ignorance. Many people are ashamed to admit that they do not know something, and by such pride forfeit the opportunity to learn, but not Thomas—he unabashedly acknowledged he was in the dark.

Then again, even at the most famous moment of his life, Thomas revealed certain strengths as well as weaknesses. Admittedly, he had taken a negative position on the claim of resurrection, but in his favor is the fact that he did change when the evidence was presented to him. He was the kind of person who could alter his opinion and admit he was wrong and embrace the new light that had broken in, and this is no ordinary virtue. At least Thomas was not a rigid sort of bigot who, no matter what the facts indicate, remains entrenched in prejudice. He could turn full circle when the evidence called for it, and thus revealed a flexibility of spirit that is admirable indeed. Dr. Weatherspoon's sermon was a real eyeopener to me in terms of the larger mystery that was the disciple Thomas, and I lived for some time with this expanded image of the man.

However, some time ago, in my own devotions, I worked through the Gospel of John again and had occasion to ponder anew this man Thomas. This time yet another facet of his being, one that somehow I had never seen before, came home to me, and that was Thomas' chronic pessimism. Even in the face of his obvious loyalty and honesty and flexibility, I could not ignore the fact that Thomas invariably seemed to expect the worst out of the future. He continually faced the Great Not Yet with very little positive openness to what might happen, and with a lot of negative presumptions about what was going to be.

For example, his words about accompanying Jesus back to Jerusalem have a bitter, fatalistic ring to them: "Let us also go, that we may die with him" (John 11:16, KJV). The spirit here seems to be more one of exasperation and despair rather than deep commitment and companionship. Thomas was not saying, "I see what you are attempting and, dangerous as it is, I want to risk it with you." He rather seems to have been saying, "The whole thing is suicidal. Nothing good can possibly come of it. We might as well face facts; this movement has had it. Let's resign ourselves to the worst." Of course, in point of fact, Thomas did not die alongside Jesus in an act of total loyalty. He, like the other eleven, abandoned our Lord at the crucial moment and fled for safety, perhaps saying all along, "I knew it. I could have told you. The worst is bound to happen."

This same pessimistic strain can be seen in the other episodes about Thomas. When Jesus assumed the disciples understood about his going to the Father, Thomas not only denied the fact but cast some doubt on whether they were capable of such understanding. The question, "How can we know?", may have been more of a negative assumption than a cry for help. He may have been saying, "Such knowledge is beyond us. Why do you keep expecting more of us than we can possibly achieve?"

This same negativism is evident also in the post-Resurrection scenes. When told by the other disciples that Jesus had in fact arisen, Thomas stated unequivocally that he did not believe them and would not until he saw the wounds with his own eyes and touched them with his own hands. Now, obviously, Thomas did not expect these conditions to be met. The statement he made was his way of saying no to what seemed to him to be an utter impossibility. No one could have been more profoundly shocked than was Thomas when Jesus did meet his challenge head-on and gave him exactly the kind of evidence he had demanded. It is clear from the passage that Thomas was utterly overwhelmed with awe and surprise at what stood before him. Pessimist that he was, he had never dared dream that something like this was possible in our kind of world. His proclivity to expect the worst and to view the future with apprehension was overwhelmingly evident right to the end.

As I said earlier, this is a side of Thomas that I had never detected before, and it made a deep impression on me, just as his stance as a doubter had impressed me earlier. For once again I suppose "like attracts like—it takes one to know one." The pessimism I saw in Thomas resonated with something deep inside me. What I am saying is that most people I know, myself included, share something of Thomas's tendency to expect the worst out of the future. Our stance toward what is to be is neither very open nor very hopeful. We tend to assume that things are going to go from bad to worse. We are living in a time of deep depression and negativism, and I believe that at the bottom of it all is Thomas's spirit-problem—the habit of expecting the worst, of looking to the future in despair, of assuming that bad things are sure to be. The temptation to despair of the future is a temptation every one of us faces every day.

What can we say about this problem in light of the Christian gospel? Well, first of all, we can say that it has a tremendous effect on the quality of life we lead. Expecting the worst is not merely a neutral attitudinal stance— one among many an individual may choose—but a creative stance that goes a long way to actually shaping the form the future will have for us. This is the dark side of the "self-fulfilling prophecies" I mentioned in the previous chapter. We humans internalize in our behavioral patterns not only our motivations but also our expectations, which means that if we expect the worst we actually create a set of conditions that help the worst to come into existence.

For example, if I think of a problem as insoluble and only capable of getting worse, my very expectation will immobilize whatever energies I might have to work toward an answer. Eric Fromm fears that this is what is happening to modern people in the face of problems like war and overpopulation and the future of our cities. In spite of dire predictions and much discussion of the problems, precious little is really being done to meet these challenges. It is almost as if, way down deep, we have already concluded that catastrophe is inevitable and that therefore all efforts to avert it are futile. Such expections, mind you, can become self-fulfilling prophecies. The very inactivity which such pessimism produces becomes itself a factor in the breakdown of the future. This is why I say chronic pessimism is not just a neutral stance. It becomes a potent force in producing the very negativism it expects, and so becomes part of a vicious cycle that sucks people and institutions down to their destruction.

This is what needs to be said *about* the kind of pessimism that was so manifest in Thomas. Now the question arises: What can we say *to* it as Christians? It is significant to me that Jesus rebuked Thomas for his attitude in the upper room. He was not condemning Thomas for wanting evidence on which to base his conclusions; that was not the issue at all. He was rather rebuking Thomas for his prejudicial, negative spirit, for drawing conclusions about realities he had never seen. Thomas had been projecting on the Great Not Yet certain limits and expectations that were not justified. After all, he had not yet experienced the mystery of the future. How can a mortal man, who does not even fully comprehend what has happened in the past, dare lay hold of the future and say dogmatically what can or cannot be? Human finitude demands that we be more humble than that before the mystery of life, and that we leave words like *possible* and *impossible* to the vocabulary of God. We are simply not in a position to be definitive about the future.

What I am saying is that the kind of pessimism we see in Thomas is downright presumptuous. It is claiming to know more about the Not Yet than any person has a right to claim, for, after all, we have not visited the future nor even plumbed the depths of present reality. Anyone who has lived very long in this world is bound to have been radically surprised again and again by the turn of events.

I could cite you any number of situations that have

turned out quite different from what I could have dreamed from the perspective of certain moments. For instance, I have a very close friend who years ago seemed to absolutely hit bottom in his personal and professional life. He lost his job, broke up with the girl he loved and planned to marry, and for a time appeared to have flunked life altogether. That was only fourteen years ago. Today that man is a respected political figure, gaining stature each year on the national scene. I often think, "If anyone had told me back in 1957 what is today an actuality, I would have laughed at him or her." If ever the word *impossible* would have seemed humanly justifiable, it would have been in relation to that man's prospects of being elected to anything.

Experiences like this are what have taught me to shun dogmatic pessimism, for life is simply too mysterious and too full of surprises to speak definitely about what has not yet happened. In the name of humility alone, Thomas had no right to his negative perspective. But an even stronger reason against such pessimism is the perspective of faith that comes to us out of the biblical revelation. On this basis, one could go further than saying pessimism is presumptuous. In light of the God of Abraham and Isaac and Jacob, it is downright heretical!

If we take at all seriously the vision of life given to us in the Bible, we have to look to the future not only in openness but in hopefulness as well. Why do I say this? Because the God disclosed in the Bible is both the Source and the Fulfiller of all creation. He did not begin this world carelessly or irresponsibly. He is not the kind of God to start something and then lose interest in it or to find he is incapable of completing it. No, he is the one who is both willing and able to finish the good project he began back at the beginning. This is what the flow of history is all about—a movement from incompleteness toward fulfillment.

I am not sure how many people have ever really

grasped the decisive image of history that is central to the Bible. In fact, many people seem to conclude from the Genesis accounts that perfection was created back in the beginning, and that history has been nothing but a steady process of falling away from Paradise. If this is our vision, no wonder the future seems so foreboding. No wonder the thrust of life becomes to get back to some former state rather than to move forward into the Not Yet Known.

I am convinced such a retrogressive image is the opposite of biblical truth. The Paradise stories of Genesis are the infancy narratives of history, not pictures of the finished product. Something was begun back then that was full of potential but not yet completed; this is why God invited human beings to collaborate with him in finishing the world that was just being born. The subduing of the earth, the gaining of dominion over the elements, the naming of the animals—none of this implies a static perfection already completed, but a momentous adventure just beginning. The God of the Bible is always pictured as out ahead of us—as he was ahead of Abraham and Moses—inviting us to join him in creative venture. Perfection in the biblical framework is always in the future, not in the past. Our destination is not Eden and the innocence of infancy, but rather New Jerusalem, the City of God, where all of the potentiality of creation will finally be pulled together and brought to its wholeness by the Author and Perfector of all things.

It is this biblical frame of reference that gives us a basis for openness and hopefulness toward the future. The agonies of history which we are now experiencing are to be understood as growing pains, not the pangs of death, for history is in God's hands. We can look forward not to a decline from perfection into disintegration, but rather to an incline from incompleteness to fulfillment.

This is why I said earlier that ultimate despair is not

just humanly presumptuous; it is biblically heretical. Thomas's habit of always expecting the worst stands in glaring contrast to the way of biblical faith, so no wonder Jesus set himself over against Thomas in their show-down. Our Lord's own way of approaching life was radically different from that of his pessimistic disciple. He really understood the faith of his fathers, and therefore knew how to look toward the future in openness and hopefulness. His public ministry began on a note of positive anticipation: "The time is fulfilled, and the kingdom of God is at hand; repent, and believe in the gospel" (Mark 1:15). And this kind of forward-looking spirit characterized all his life, even the last days when the shadow of the cross loomed so large before him, Jesus' attitude in going up to Jerusalem was very different from that of Thomas! He had all kinds of forebodings and certainly did not look forward to the coming time as to some kind of joyous lark. Yet he believed it was part of God's purpose, a means of maturing and perfecting the world, and so he approached it with profound hopefulness as well as foreboding. He was convinced that good would come out of this ordeal, and that is what he kept telling his disciples—a far cry from Thomas's bitter "Let's go up with him and die and get it over with." The one who could say, with his last breath, "Father, into thy hands I commend my spirit," is a man of hope, not of despair, and this is the one who brought the faith of Israel to its fullest expression—our Savior, our Lord, our Example.

It is in contrast to Jesus, then, that the pessimism of Thomas is seen for what it really is and thereby judged. To expect the worst, to be sure that what is coming is less than what has gone by, to project negative limits onto the future—this is humanly presumptuous, for it is claiming more than we have a right to claim from our actual experience, and it is religiously heretical, for it violates the biblical image of God as the Source and Fulfiller of history. The God of the Bible knows what he is doing. He did not create a perfect world, only to stand by helpless and indifferent as it gradually disintegrates before his eyes. Rather, he created a world of rich beginnings, and he labors even now to finish it, to perfect it, to mature it. And he calls us to help him in this venture. This is how the agonies of our time are to be interpreted. They are birth pangs, growing pains, and, according to Saint Paul, are "not worth comparing with the glory that is to be revealed to us" (Rom. 8:18). Blessed is the person who lives by that hope, even though it is not yet perfectly clear exactly what is to come.

The whole point I am trying to make is that Christianity is a way of openness and hope, not a way of despair and inaction, and my friendship with Thomas has helped make this truth clearer to me. I am therefore indebted to him once again, for he has been my teacher—even though, in this case, through a negative example. Yet remember, Thomas did change at the end. In the presence of the risen Christ himself, Thomas fell in utter awe, which means faith can be born in the heart of the doubter and hope in the heart of even the most dogmatic pessimist.

10

A MINISTRY OF LIBERATION

Matthew 25:31–46; Luke 13:10–17

ONE OF THE MOST PROBING PASSAGES in all the Gospels is Jesus' parable of the Last Judgment, found in Matthew 25. This parable, with its arresting image of the Son of man dividing all the people of the earth "as a shepherd divideth his sheep from the goats," is basically concerned with what the criteria for judgment at this Final Examination of history will be. When we are each called before our Creator to give an account of our lives, what will he want to know? The parable of the Last Judgment suggests it will be this: How did we relate to the hungry, the thirsty, the stranger, the naked, the sick, the imprisoned—in short, to the least of our brothers and sisters on earth?

To the degree that one has paid attention to the whole sweep of biblical religion, such a question will come as no surprise. It was evident from the very foundational event—the deliverance of Israel from Egypt—that this God of the Bible was most unusual, in that he was con-

cerned for those at the "tail-end" of the human proces-
sion. From this event the conviction grew that God was a
Father as well as a Creator, which means he had love for
all he had made and was like any good parent in being
especially concerned for those who were having the most
difficulties.

Jesus was the explosion into history of this very God of
the Old Testament who cared about the weakest and
most lowly of his children. Jesus was both aware of and
responsive to the least one of his brothers and sisters
who was hungry, or thirsty, or naked, or a stranger, or
sick, or imprisoned; in fact, relating to them was the central thrust of his life. Just as the God of the Old Testament dropped back to the tail-end of the human proces-
sion—to Israel in Egypt—to show his concern, so Jesus
dropped back to the last and the least among those he encountered and focused on them his best and his most. In
fact, the events listed in the parable of the Last Judgment
could almost be used to sum up what Jesus did with his
days and nights on earth.

This is why I believe this parable is so important. In a
way, it is a preview of the Test that is to come for all of us
at the end of history. Yet again, like any good exam, it is
also a review, a kind of summary of what the course has
been all about. As succinctly as anywhere in all the Bible,
the parable of the Last Judgment shows us what God is
like, why he does what he does, and what he expects of
us who are made in his image. It is full of implications for
the way we live our lives, the way we minister or fail to
minister to those around us. In this chapter, I would like
to focus on the last category Jesus mentions in the parable: "I was in prison, and ye came unto me. . . . Inasmuch as ye have done it unto one of the least of these my
brethren, ye have done it unto me" (Matt. 25:36,40, KJV).

In a very real sense, the parable would be incomplete
without this category, for in trying to comprehend both

the problems we humans are up against and the ministry of Jesus, this matter of imprisonment cannot be overlooked. At its deepest level, it is something more than the experience of being in a jail, although that may be the most dramatic form of imprisonment. Actually, imprisonment occurs any time an individual is stifled or prevented from actualizing his or her potential. What we are talking about here is the tragedy that results when human beings are prevented from bringing to fulfillment all that is within them to be.

In this sense, we are all imprisoned to one degree or another, and Jesus seemed to look on this problem as one of the central challenges of his ministry. In fact, when he went back to the synagogue in Nazareth to declare himself to his fellow townspeople, he chose these words from Isaiah:

> The Spirit of the Lord is upon me, because he has anointed me to preach good news to the poor. He has sent me to proclaim release to the captives and recovering of sight to the blind, to set at liberty those who are oppressed, to proclaim the acceptable year of the Lord (Luke 4:18–19).

I believe it is significant that, of the five tasks that are specified here, two are concerned with this problem of imprisonment and with how it can be overcome. There is little wonder that, down through the centuries, Jesus has come to be known as a liberator, and has even been called "the new Moses," after the image of the great Old-Testament emancipator. Liberation was a dominant characteristic of Jesus' ministry. Nothing was more disturbing to him or moved him to action more quickly than the sight of a human being who, in one form or another, was being shackled or stifled from becoming what God made him or her to be.

If we are to share this concern and learn how to participate with Christ in the ministry of liberation—as the parable of the Last Judgment clearly indicates we are to do—we need to look more deeply at the problem and find out just what is involved here. We need to ask how people ever come to be enslaved in the first place. Who is to blame here? What are the forces we are up against when we confront the problem of imprisonment?

As I mentioned in an earlier chapter, my own understanding of just how complicated this subject really is has grown across the years. I used to think rather simplistically about the problem of imprisonment; I assumed that everybody wanted to be free, and that it was only the will to dominate on the part of certain tyrants that stood in the way of freedom for everyone. To put the matter in the images of Israel's experience in Egypt, I used to put all the blame for Israel's enslavement on Pharoah. Here was one who wanted to engage in a massive building program to enhance his own reputation, and he needed lots of cheap labor, so he took the foreigners in the land, the descendants of Jacob and Joseph, and proceeded to reduce them to the level of chattel property. With superior force, he made them serve his selfish purposes, at an incredible expense to their own personhoods.

This is precisely how I used to account for all experiences of human imprisonment—some power-thirsty force superimposing its will on a freedom-loving but weaker party. And, to be sure, the will to tyrannize is almost always a factor when enslavement occurs. But I have lately come to see that this is by no means the whole story or even the most crucial factor.

If you read further in the account of Israel's deliverance from Egypt, you will discover a very different challenge to freedom, one that was internal rather than external. I'm speaking about the unwillingness of the children of Israel to bear the responsibility of freedom. You see, all Moses' problems did not disappear when he finally got

96

across the Red Sea and away from Pharoah. There, in the desert, where at last the Israelites could breathe the air of liberty, they began to discover the burden of freedom, the complexity of deciding things for themselves. They began to realize that, while slavery had had many serious disadvantages, at least it had offered a security of sorts. After all, being controlled by someone else can be stifling, but it also simplifies things immeasurably. Because the children of Israel found it hard to cope with freedom, Moses had as much trouble with those who wanted to go back to the dependence of Egypt as he had had with those who had worked to keep them there by force.

This is the other side of the imprisonment problem— one that has to be taken into account if we are to understand the whole situation. If we would be liberators, we need to realize that the will to dominate is not the only enemy of freedom. The willingness to be dominated, to hand over freedom in return for security, is another possible explanation for enslavement. Sadly enough, many people find the burden of freedom too heavy and the demands of choice too great, and they voluntarily choose the simplicity of prison over the bracing atmosphere of liberty.

This is important to recognize, for it means that the ministry of liberation will need to involve an internal challenge to an imprisoned person to accept the responsibility of freedom, as well as the external challenge to a tyrant to relinquish domination. In fact, the realization that the problem of imprisonment is made up of both factors is often the turning point in realistic liberation. Thomas Ogletree says that one of the most significant moments in the American civil rights movement occurred in 1960, when a group of Black students at The American Seminary in Nashville held a service of repentance for "the sin of acquiescence." According to Ogletree, this service marked the realization that, as bad as white racism might be, it was not the whole problem. Blacks had been willing in many instances to deny their humanity and to let others make all their decisions for them, and it was this willingness to relinquish freedom, as well as the White will to dominate, that had to be attacked if real freedom were to emerge.

Here, then, are the twin problems that the condition of imprisonment poses for any would-be liberator. How did Jesus, "the new Moses," respond to them? I think we can get a significant glimpse into both his heart and his strategy by looking at the incident recorded in Luke 13:10–17. Jesus is teaching in a synagogue on the Sabbath when a grotesquely crippled woman appears. She is described by Luke as having "a spirit of infirmity" which caused her to be bent double, unable to stand up straight. In another place, Jesus speaks of her as having been "bound by Satan for eighteen years." Here is a classic example of imprisonment, of a person not being able to fulfill her potential because of the forces which shackled her and held her back.

How had she gotten in such a condition? We are not told specifically, of course. But it could well be that as a young woman she, like so many other young people, may have ventured out toward actualizing her freedom, only to experience failure and humiliation and lose all sense of self-worth. Just as the Prodigal found the burden of freedom too heavy in the far country and wanted to come back home and be dependent as a hired servant, so perhaps this one recoiled from responsibility, shrank back both inwardly and outwardly, and tried to become small again. In mental hospitals, it is not at all uncommon for sick people to double up and assume a fetal position, symbolizing with their bodies the state of dependency and external control to which they long to return. It may sound a bit far-fetched, but I feel that, in much the same way, the bent-over position of this woman's body may have symbolized the state of her spirit. She just may have become bound to powers of destruction by being unwilling to accept responsibility for her own existence.

At any rate, Jesus was moved with compassion at the sight of such boundness, and he proceeded to do several things that resulted in the miracle of her release. For one thing, he showed love for her by noticing her and speaking to her individually and touching her. I wonder how long it had been since anyone outside the family had paid any attention to this crumpled heap of a woman? Her own sense of worthlessness may well have been reinforced daily as everyone ignored her or avoided her. Yet suddenly here was One who saw her and spoke to her, and who by this simple act conveyed the fact that he felt she had worth. What was happening to her seemed to matter to him—enough, in fact, for him to stop what he was doing and concentrate on her as if there were no one else in the world. First, then, was a simple act of love.

Another thing Jesus did was to bring a word of hope into the woman's life. Out of the clear blue sky, with great authority, he declared that she did not have to go on like she was forever, that she could be freed from her infirmity. Second only to this woman's sense of worthlessness must have been her sense of hopelessness. After eighteen years, what could she expect except more of the same? The horizon of life probably had closed in gradually on her until she no longer awoke in the morning open to any new possibility or prospect. Then suddenly Jesus came and shouted "No!" to the idea that this woman's past needed to be the measure of her future. "You can be freed, made straight again"—that was a prospect that had not dawned on her in years, yet was indispensable to the event of her liberation.

A third thing Jesus did, however, must have had equal significance for this bent-over woman, for it was an act of faith that gave her a whole new way to see herself and to live her life. Jesus called her "a daughter of Abraham." Now, on the surface these words may not seem very significant, but to her they carried deep and life-changing undertones. Through them, Jesus was actually reminding her all over again who she was by the grace of creation. He was saying, in effect, "You belong to the people of God; you do not belong to Satan. You are by nature a child of the God of Abraham and Isaac and Jacob, the God who made you and loves you and wants you to be yourself." And because Jesus had the unique power of being able to get inside people and make them feel again their relation to God, something truly wonderful happened to this bent-over one. Just like the Prodigal Son, in that moment she seems to have "come to herself," and to have remembered all over again who she really was—a daughter of Abraham, a child of God. Out of this realization she found the power to do something she had not been able to do for years—she stood up straight and held her head high and began to walk about freely as a person of worth and value! In a moment, she was loosed, liberated from imprisonment, set free to fulfill herself.

It is right at this point that the secret of Jesus' liberating power can best be understood. In my judgment, it always involves the realization of two things: one, that a person belongs to God alone and is dependent only on him, and two, that this God on whom one depends wants that person to be himself or herself and nothing else. These are the foundation stones out of which all personal freedom comes. And if you dig behind them a bit, it is not hard to understand why they are so vital.

For one thing, it is simply a statement of fact that we are controlled by those things on which we depend. If I think of myself as belonging to a certain reality and drawing my life from this source, then what that reality demands of me is going to be crucial in the shaping of my being. It is everlastingly true that "he who pays the piper calls the tune." I have referred in an earlier chapter to Keith Miller's helpful insight that we all play our lives to some audience, to some person or organization or group of people whose approval we really want. These are the people who really affect our lives, and their likes and dislikes have powerful impact on our behavior.

It is in this context that we can see why Jesus' words to the woman about belonging to the God of Abraham were so crucial. The truth is, this God is the only Reality in all the world who knows and loves us just as we are individually, and who wants us to be nothing but ourselves! You can mark it down as an external axiom that if you take your pay from any source other than God, the tune you will pipe will not be your tune in all its fullness, for your uniqueness will be ignored and twisted around and distorted to suit the needs of another. Such distortion is what happens to people who allow themselves to belong to anything other than God. For, I repeat: only he knows us and loves us for what we are. After all, he is the one who made us! If he is "paying us to pipe," the tune he will call is the melody of our own unique selves, and this is liberation of the highest sort. To belong to anything else in the world is to be bound and hemmed in, but to belong to the God who made us and loves us and glories in our uniqueness is to be liberated, for *in his will is our peace, our wholeness, and in his service is perfect freedom.*

Here, then, is how Jesus worked a miracle of liberation. He saw full well that the problem of imprisonment is twofold, that there are always foes without who would tyrannize, but also foes within who would have us capitulate. To one who was shackled by both of these, he acted in love and in hope and in faith, and in so doing he loosed her from her bond and freed her to stand up straight, to walk with head high as a daughter of Abraham and a child of God.

Two questions remain. First, has the liberation of Jesus

ever happened to you? It can, just as surely and realistically as it happened to the bent-over woman. Second, if it has, are you on a mission with Christ to liberate others? Jesus' ministry of liberation started with his being aware of the imprisoned about him and wanting to help. That day in the synagogue Jesus saw the crippled woman, and that was the beginning. We all need to be more aware of the bound people all about us. Someday he is going to ask us about this, and we do not want to have to answer in astonishment, "When did I see you in prison, Lord?"

11

CASTING OUT FEAR

1 John 1:5–7; 4:14–19

BACK IN THE FIFTIES, during my student days, I once spent an entire summer traveling through Europe living on a shoestring. One evening I stopped at a tiny village inn not too far from London. The room was small and simply appointed, and the first thing that caught my eye was an inscription that had been carved in the mantle over the fireplace. It read like this: "Fear knocked at the door. Faith answered. There was no one there." Those words made a deep impression on me, and since that summer I have thought of them often, but my conclusions about them have gone through some changes over the years.

My initial reaction to that inscription was to say categorically that it was not true. There are many occasions, I reasoned, when fear knocks at the door and you answer and there *is* something there—a threat that sends shudders of terror through your whole being. After all, this world in which we find ourselves is not some disaster-proof paradise; there are diseases that cripple and kill, sadistic people who hurt and destroy, catastrophes that turn our lives upside down. Therefore, I thought, it would be a grave mistake to dismiss or ignore our experiences of fear.

I felt we would be far better served if we looked on fear as one of the good gifts of God—a built-in, automatic, and wonderfully dependable alarm system that alerts us to the presence of danger. If I am walking through the woods and suddenly hear an ominous rattle, then look down to see a snake coiled and ready to strike, I do not have to say to my body, "Get scared, Baby, it is time to be frightened!" The job of getting scared has already been done for me, and in the process extra energy has been mobilized that will enable me to meet the crisis. We humans probably could not survive for long without this fear mechanism, I argued; to be without fear would mean to live without defenses, and that is not desirable in this dangerous world. So I found myself at first disagreeing with what I thought that mantelpiece inscription was saying about fear—that all fear experiences are based on illusions.

However, as I continued to turn this matter over in my mind, my initial absolutism began to crumble. As I looked back to the times when I had experienced fear, I could see that very often the words of the inscription had been true! That is, my fear had not originated in some obvious, visible threat, but had arisen from within me and been projected onto external reality. Of course, there had been times when I was faced with a real threat and my fears were created *for* me by outside events. But in many instances I had been the one doing the creating; the movement of fear had been from inside to outside.

As I thought along these lines, I remembered something that had happened during the Thanksgiving holiday when I was a senior at Baylor University. Almost everyone else had gone home, but it was too far and too expensive for me to travel from Texas to Tennessee, so I had stayed in the dorm. All my roommates were gone; in fact, I doubt if there were three people in all of Brooks Hall. About two o'clock that Saturday night, I was abruptly awakened by a loud knocking at my door. When I realized I was not dreaming and that I was alone in that huge dormitory, a sense of sheer terror swept over me. I began to think, "Who on earth could this be in the middle of the night? Am I about to be robbed or kidnapped?" In my terror all kinds of possibilities flashed through my mind. Should I try to escape by jumping out the window? That was a less than desirable option, since my room was on the third floor. Should I barricade myself in the bathroom and hope that two locks would succeed if one failed?

Finally, I managed to creep to the door, and cracked it ever so slightly. There, to my great relief, stood one of my best friends. He had decided to come back a day early and was locked out of his room; he simply wanted a bed for the rest of the night. You see, there had been no real threat on the other side of that door. The terror I had experienced from the moment I awakened until I finally opened the door was entirely of my own making. It was what I had done to an event, rather than what an event had done to me.

As I reflected along this line, I was amazed to discover that a large percentage of my fearing is of this nature. When something happens, I do not go to the door and face up squarely to what is knocking; instead, I "distress myself with vain imaginings" as the poem, "Desiderata," puts it, and project onto the knock far more than is actually there. Such a practice is destructive in two ways. It not only produces a lot of unnecessary anguish—for much that we imagine never comes true—but it also can drive us to act very unwisely in response to fanciful fears.

I said a few moments ago, partly in jest, that one of the things I thought of that night in my dorm room was jumping out of a third-story window. But tragically enough, things even worse than this have been done before the true nature of what was knocking has been determined. Years ago I had to conduct the funeral of a man who had taken his own life. In the note he left his family, he explained that he had discovered a painful lump in his side a few days before and had remembered that both of his parents had died of cancer. "I cannot go through all that suffering," he concluded. "I'm taking the easy way out." The tragedy of this was that he took this extreme measure without ever seeing a doctor! The autopsy required by the state showed that the mass in his side was in fact benign and could have been removed.

Now, admittedly, this is an extreme example. But think of the times we have let the unknown send us into panic. Something happens, and instead of "going to the door" and directly confronting the actual reality, we let our anxieties run wild. We imagine the worst, and then we often react, not to what is really there, but to the terrible things we have concocted in our imaginations.

According to Genesis, one of the reasons our world is in such a mess roots back to this very kind of mishandling of fear. The first man and woman are pictured as living in a kind of unbroken harmony with all of reality. Then a serpent appeared and proceeded to give a certain kind of knock on the door of these human creatures. He aroused a sense of anxiety in them by insinuating that they did not know what they were doing, that they were not OK as they were, but were only a fraction of what they could be. Then the serpent identified God as the culprit. He laid the blame squarely on the Creator, claiming God had lied to the creatures about the forbidden fruit. They would not die if they ate it, said the serpent. On the contrary, their eyes would be opened; they would be able to determine right and wrong for themselves, and they would become gods in their own right.

This encounter left the man and woman profoundly confused, to say the least. It was their first experience with the anxiety that grows out of uncertainty, with a "knock" that they did not fully understand. How tragic it is that they chose to respond as they did. You see, if they had gone to that door and taken their uncertainty straight to the Reality in question, the outcome would have been different. I am certain that if they had asked God directly about the serpent's charges, he would have been able to allay their fears. If they had just so much as opened the door, if they had looked God in the face and asked him what he was really up to in all this creating, they would have seen the positive Joy that is the source of everything, and they would not have been afraid anymore.

But the tragedy of all tragedies is that they did not answer the door! Instead of finding out for themselves about God's true nature, they jumped to a conclusion about him that had no basis in fact, and proceeded in panic to do to themselves what the man with the lump in his side had done—to act self-destructively.

Unfortunately, this way of handling fear got started early in the human drama, and we have all been affected by it, but it does not have to be our pattern if we don't want it to be. I once heard Dr. John DeFoore say that we have *to learn* to handle fear creatively, that it is not an instinct born within us. This means that early in life we all begin to develop ways of coping with fearful situations, and that the methods we develop may not always be healthy ones. But it also means that these self-destructive reactions to fear are something we can *unlearn!* We can learn new tactics if we find our old ones are not working for us.

This is an area of existence in which I myself am trying to do some work just now. To be honest, I find it to be a painful and demanding discipline. For one thing, I did not realize how big a part fear played in my life until I began to get in touch with my true feelings.

Hugh Missildine says that fear is one of the earliest emotions a baby experiences, and that all fears tend to be variations of three basic ones: the fear of falling, the fear of loud noises, and the fear of being abandoned. I not only remember having felt each of these fears as a child, but I still experience them in more sophisticated form to this day. For example, the fear of falling translates, when one becomes an adult, into the fear of failing—the fear of losing one's place or one's job or the esteem of others. I have known this fear in its various forms across the years. At other times I have been afraid of being overwhelmed by the "loud noise" of some catastrophe like a depression or a tornado or a crippling illness. Then, too, there is the recurring fear of abandonment, the fear that the resources which now support me will evaporate and I will be left alone and bereft. The particular form this fear takes for me as it affects my professional life is the fear that the springs of creativity will dry up, that there will come a Sunday morning when I have to preach and I will have nothing to say.

I am guessing that what I am describing here is not foreign to most of you. In one form or another, the fears of falling or failing, of loud noises and catastrophes, or abandonment or being forsaken are things that come knocking on the doors of all our lives.

And let me confess that learning "to go to the door" and answer my fears is one of the biggest single challenges I face. My tendency is to give way to all kinds of "imaginings," to assume the worst and begin to act on that basis rather than to face up to the real situation and then decide what to do. Intellectually, I know that "the good news comes by facing up to the bad news," but at the emotional level I am often a coward; my tendency is either to do nothing and hope the knock will go away or to escape in panic by jumping out the nearest window. It is a matter of conscious relearning for me to discipline my "imaginings," to make sure my fears are based on what is outside the door rather than what is inside. This involves going against the grain of a lifelong habit of creating rather than responding to fears, but I am convinced it is the only way to handle this part of life constructively.

Let me go on to say that the greatest single help I have found in learning to "answer the door" has been the perspective of biblical religion. The influence of this way of looking at life finally led me to my third conclusion about that inscription over the fireplace—that, in an ultimate sense, the inscription is always completely true! This represented coming full circle for me. I started out saying "not so" to those words, then moved to saying "sometimes so" and then finally to saying "ultimately so." What changed me? It finally got through to me that 1 John 1:5 is true, that "God is light, and in him is no darkness at all" (KJV). This means that the ultimate source of our existence is something good and not bad, and that, while all kinds of painful and harmful things can be done to us here, none of these things has the power to sever our ties with God or separate us from him. It is in this sense that we can truthfully say, "Fear knocked at the door. Faith answered. There was no one there." In other words, there is nothing at the door that has the power totally to destroy us.

Some time ago I was profoundly moved by reading Eugene O'Neill's beautiful play, *Lazarus Laughed*, which describes what life was like for the brother of Mary and Martha after Jesus called him back from the grave. There were many changes in his behavior, but the most important thing was that *he was not afraid anymore*. He had experienced the worst, and it had not destroyed him or swept him out of God's hands. Thus, he was able to "answer the door" with confidence. His one message to everyone was, "Don't be afraid. There is only life. There is only God. There is nothing ultimately to fear," and as such Lazarus was an utterly free man.

You see, the only thing that can finally cast out fear is Perfect Love, and this is what comes to us through the pages of the Bible. The serpent long ago was absolutely and totally wrong. And when men and women refused to move close to God and find out that truth for themselves, lo and behold, he proceeded to move closer to them, to show them their fears were unfounded. This is what the whole story of the Bible is about.

When God finally found me and reconciled me to his goodness, I reached a turning point in my ongoing battle with fear. Do not get me wrong—I still find myself frightened by much that comes to me in life. There are all kinds of mysterious "knockings in the night" that fill me with foreboding. But when I remember what the real situation is—that "God is light and in him is no darkness at all," that this kind of power encircles the whole of creation, then I am given the courage to "answer the door" and face whatever is there. Often what I find is not nearly as bad as I imagined, and what filled me with terror turns out to be a friend. But even if the presence at the door turns out to be a foe, there is only so much he can do to me. He cannot destroy what is most important about me—my rootage in God, the source of all life and joy. Martin Luther said heroically when it seemed all the world was arrayed against him, "Let goods and kindred go, this mortal life also. The body they may kill. God's truth abideth still." This is the kind of faith that old inscription is talking about. And when fear knocks and you answer with this sort of reality, then it is true that there is no one there!

12

A PATTERN FOR COPING

Mark 6:30–44

SOME TIME AGO, a highly placed public-health official spoke at the University of Kentucky on the controversial subject of drug usage. He openly acknowledged that, at that time, "the jury [was] still out" as to all the physical effects of using a drug like marijuana. (Since then, research has indicated that long-term use of marijuana does indeed cause physical damage.) However, he went on to say that "the jury [was] already back in" as to the ways such a habit affects the personality. He wisely noted that learning to cope with difficulty is one of life's most crucial lessons, and that the pattern of coping one develops early in life goes a long way toward shaping one's whole personality. This is why the use of mind-altering or mood-altering drugs can be so damaging, especially to young people. In a word, drugs offer an escape from reality. "Getting high" is really another form of something very, very old—the practice of running away from things as they are into a region of contrived fantasy.

The speaker underlined the fact that this could be the most damaging aspect of the drug phenomena, for, while we do not yet know all marijuana does to our physical cells, we *do* know something of what it does to the human spirit; it encourages a strategy of escape as the way of coping with difficulty. If this be the case, then, long after the use of drugs themselves is discontinued, "the melody will linger on," and it will be a sad one, for escapism is an inadequate way of coping with life. The person who persists in trying to escape reality will only descend further and further into helplessness.

I, for one, found this speech to be a very wise word on the whole troubled subject of drug abuse. What I especially liked was the way the official went to the heart of the matter. Rather than moralizing around the edges, he raised one of life's primary concerns—learning to cope with difficulty—and then he identified drug usage for what it is—an inadequate means of coping that creates more problems than it solves. As I thought about what he said, however, I found myself wishing he had gone even further, for his words led me to ask a deeper question: What is a healthy answer to this problem of coping? It is all well and good to speak negatively and say that drugs are not the answer, but that is not enough. What we need is a positive word—a constructive model that shows us how the problems of life might be faced and successfully managed.

Quite predictably, because I am a Christian, I turned to the figure of Christ to see what I could find in terms of a model for coping. It was not long until I was pondering one of the most famous events in his life—the time he fed the five thousand in the wilderness. This episode must have made a deep impression on the disciples, for it is the only miracle in the whole ministry of Jesus that all four of the Gospels record. The outline of the story was familiar to me, of course, but at this reading I was surprised to discover just how relevant it is to this particular issue of coping with life's difficulties. This story depicts Jesus really up against a problem, and the way he responded is worthy of our most careful consideration.

Perhaps a word about the background of the event will set the whole picture in better perspective. At this time, Jesus and his disciples were trying to get away to themselves so they could reflect on the mission the Twelve had just completed. Galilee was a crowded, densely populated country, so they had crossed the Sea of Galilee to the more sparsely inhabited eastern shore. But the people who had been following them saw them embarking in their boats and ran around the nothern end of the Sea. When Jesus and his friends arrived, there facing them were the same pleading multitudes.

One of the wonders about Jesus was that he never looked on needy human beings as a nuisance! Instead, out of deep compassion, he rearranged his plans and worked with them all day. His disciples were hardly as flexible or generous in their attitudes, and by late afternoon they had "had it up to here" with the crowd and wanted to be rid of them. They also realized that the people were hungry and tired, and that crowds in this condition can get hostile and out of hand. So they pulled Jesus aside and pointed out the difficulty, suggesting that he disperse the people quickly before things went from bad to worse. It was a perfectly natural suggestion in the face of what Jesus and the disciples were facing—a bona fide problem situation, full of stress and potential danger. But watch closely how Jesus proceeded to cope with the problem, for his is the positive model about which I spoke.

It seems to me Jesus' approach involved three significant steps. First, he refused the disciples' suggestion that they employ the strategy of escapism; he decided instead to face the situation squarely and openly. Instead of saying, "Trouble is coming; let's go our way and let them go theirs," he said, "We are involved in this event together. In fact, I am partly responsible for their being here this late. This is not a buck we can afford to pass. We must do something about this problem of hunger and the late hour. Give them something to eat." It is clear from this reaction that, for Jesus, *the way out was always the way through*. To him, the solution of a problem never lay behind him or off on a tangent somewhere; it lay straight on the other side of the difficulty.

Initially, then, Jesus chose to cope, not to run. The second thing he did was to survey the resources inherent in the situation. He asked the disciples to do something that, in their hurry to escape the problem, they had not even thought of—to find out what they had going for them. It was actually a most reasonable request to make, and the disciples were amazed to discover that, although it was not much, there was some food available in the group—five loaves and two fishes, to be exact.

The third and climactic step in the process came when Jesus took the available resources in hand and, without anxiety or panic, began the task of meeting the hunger of the crowd. It sounds so simple to say that he began to do the best he could with what he had, and yet that was the hinge on which the whole process turned. For you know as well as I what happened when he launched out in this way—*somehow that little became enough!* What had seemed so impossible to the disciples as they looked only at the problem became a possibility through the courage and decisiveness of Jesus. He was not immobilized by the seeming disproportion of the need to the resources there at the start; he knew that nothing can begin unless that first step is taken. So, to the amazement of everybody present, Jesus began to act on the basis of what he had. And, lo and behold, his action gathered strength from all directions and turned a seemingly insoluble problem into a triumph.

How are we to regard an event of this kind? Is what happened here so utterly miraculous that we cannot relate to it, that we assume only a divine being could do this sort of thing? I realize many people look at the feeding of the five thousand this way and thus dismiss it from their lives. But I do not think this is the way Jesus would have us interpret it. After all, he became what we are—fully and completely human. He did not come to taunt us with his divinity and make us feel inferior, but to show us how the full potential of humanness could be realized. And he promised that if we learned from him we would "do greater works" than he had done (see John 14:12). Therefore, I prefer to look at this event as a concrete model of how any of us could cope with difficulty if we would.

Now, it is obvious that there is a radical difference between the way Jesus coped with difficulty there on the shores of the Sea of Galilee and the way we usually go about dealing with reality. But I believe this difference is not so much a matter of lesser capacity as it is one of unused potential. I do not believe Jesus was dazzling people with his unreachable divinity when he fed the hungry crowd; he was simply exercising full-grown humanity, something each of us has within us and is capable of developing.

For example, in this passage Jesus appears to have done something many of us have trouble doing—he came to terms with the fact that life is a process of problem solving, pure and simple. He seems to have laid aside all those childish fantasies about a place where there is no conflict or difficulty or hardship. He accepted the fact that such a region simply does not exist for us humans, and this realistic outlook enabled him to focus all his energies on the real issues of existence rather than dissipating them by trying to escape or lamenting the way things were.

I must admit that this is an area in which my tendency

differs from our Lord's. I am fifty-two years old, and I still have trouble accepting the fact that life is an unending series of problems to be faced and dealt with and solved. There is simply no escape from difficulty—anywhere, anytime, anyplace—but somehow I have trouble accepting this reality. I find myself always looking for some paradise where no demands are ever made and no hardship ever called for. This incessant search for a way to escape the inescapable and the chronic resentment of the problems that nevertheless remain are an incredible waste of energy, yet I confess that I have squandered a large portion of my life this way.

I remember that once, as a little boy, I came down with a terrible cold, and somehow I got the idea that, if I could run very fast from one room to another, I could get away from those germs the way I could get away from my puppy when I ran faster than he. My mother found me dashing from room to room, all out of breath, and when she discovered what I was attempting to do, she gently but wisely called me to reality. She explained that there are no spatial cures for a cold, that no matter where or how fast I went, the germs would go with me. "The sooner you quit trying to run away from it and start taking medicine for it, the quicker you will get well," she said.

There is a great truth here—not only for treating colds, but for all of life's problems—but I have been slow in learning it! I still have trouble accepting that life is, and always will be, a process of problem solving. I want another world, "a bed of roses," an escape from the way things are, and so I dissipate energy that could be invested in coping. In this I am different from our Lord, but the truth is, I do not have to be. I could grow up as he did; I could put away the childish things of fantasy and escapism, and settle down to the fact that life is problem solving and problem solving is life, that the only option I have is not whether to cope, but how. Problems are here to stay; the sooner I accept this fact and decide to face them, the better. Different as I am now from Jesus in the way I confront reality, I could be more like him if I would.

I could also be more like Jesus by opening my eyes to the reality that resources are always present, even in problem situations. I must admit that in a tight place I am usually like the disciples were that day by the Sea of Galilee; the vastness of the difficulty so dominates my attention that I never think of asking the positive questions. Fear has a way of making us short sighted and reducing our field of vision. Again and again, in the face of problems, I have been totally one-sided in my outlook and conceived the situation as utterly barren of positive possibilities. But, as Jesus demonstrated when he fed the five thousand, such a way of looking at things is simply unrealistic! It denies the presence of God in all that he has created, and makes him out as some remote Absentee Landlord who only intervenes from time to time.

All through his life Jesus opposed this "absentee" concept of God and affirmed God's active presence in what already existed. During the temptation experience, for example, Satan suggested that Jesus meet his need for food by having God "intervene" and make bread out of stones—implying, just like the disciples later implied, that help was to be found only outside the situation. Jesus rejected this temptation, however, and relied instead on the power of God already inherent in the seed and the earth and the process of growth. Jesus said, in effect, "I will utilize what God has already placed here rather than look only for intervention." What blindness it is to imagine any situation without some positive resources! There are always "five loaves and two fishes" in the midst of every problem, if we only have eyes to see. Of course, Jesus had such eyes and often I do not. But, again I could have eyes like his if I would let him teach me how to open mine.

The third difference between the way Jesus coped with difficulty and the way I tend to cope is to act in terms of what he had, whereas my tendency is to waver and hesitate and become increasingly immobilized. There is nothing that intensifies anxiety more than inactivity. The longer you stand still in the face of a problem, the worse it gets. By the same token, the decision to act, no matter how futile it may seem, often breaks the spell and turns the tide. The ability to start acting, even when what you can do seems only partial and you cannot see the end from the beginning, is utterly crucial in any problem-solving situation. Once again, Jesus was able to do this, and, while I most often do not, I most assuredly could, with his help—if I would.

The point I am laboring to make is simply that Jesus' pattern of coping with difficulty—radical as it may seem in comparison to our own weak ways—is not a totally impossible pattern. The things he did that day in the face of an enormous problem are things that any one of us could do if we would allow him to teach us how to cope. You see, as unnatural as it may seem to our present condition, the capacity to accept problems for what they are, to look for resources that are already there, and then to begin to act on the basis of what we have is within our potential as persons made in the image of God.

The question thus becomes: How was Jesus so able to cope? I think the secret is found in one aspect of this event that we have not yet mentioned; namely, the stance of gratitude in which Jesus received all of life in general and this event in particular. In all four of the Gospel accounts, we are told that in the midst of this crisis in the wilderness, when everybody else was wringing their hands, Jesus calmly looked up to heaven and gave thanks to God. I do not think this act pertained only to five loaves and two fish which he had found and was about to distribute. I think it included the whole of that event— life in all of its entirety as it was given to him day by day.

You see, Jesus had learned the deepest secret there is to learn—that God is good, that he who gives us our lives not only rules over us but loves us, likes us, is for us and not against us. Out of that realization came the ability to receive the events of life with gratitude, not resentment, and to regard them as expressions of mysterious love rather than as acts of hostility. He was able to see that events are God's way of dealing with us positively.

It is amazing the difference such a stance of gratitude can make in the way we cope with difficulty. If we really do begin to look on the things that happen to us as good gifts of a Father, then even the problems take on a different shape. Instead of seeing them as hopeless obstacles to our happiness, we come to see them as the challenges that give life its meaning and excitement. What would our existence be like, really, if no effort were ever called for or no challenges ever posed? Such a leveled-off existence would be intolerably boring. G. K. Chesterton was right in saying that a positive challenge is a difficulty rightly understood. Problems cease to be overwhelming when we see them as something to be received in gratitude.

The stance of thanksgiving also opens our eyes to the resources that inhere in the problems, and keeps us from ever saying, "There is nothing here that can be used." No matter how deep the crisis, God has not left that situation without its "five loaves and two fishes," and to be grateful is the way to have our eyes opened to what is already there.

Gratitude also encourages us to begin with what we have and to expect more to rise to meet us as we go. After all, what we have at the beginning has been given by a gracious God; can we not expect him to give even more to complete the task? This is what Jesus did. He began to act out in a profound sense of gratitude and such a beginning gathered up strength from earth and heaven until a multitude was fed.

I come back, then, to where I began, to that most crucial question: How do we cope with the difficulties we encounter? There are a thousand unhealthy ways of coping; taking drugs is just one of them. However, there is at least one infinitely healthy way of coping, and that is the way Jesus modeled for us on the shores of the Sea of Galilee. There, in the shadow of a great difficulty, he faced up to problems rather than running away. He laid hold of the resources already present in the situation rather than expecting outside intervention. He began to act in terms of what he had, and what he started out to do worked—powerfully and effectively.

The truth is, you can do that same thing. I can do the same thing. It is possible for all of us. How? By letting Jesus show us the Father, by letting him reconcile us to the fact that he who gives us our lives is good, by letting him teach us to receive all of life in gratitude rather than resentment. When this is our stance, the courage to cope will rise up from the depths. The problems? They will assume the shape of a challenge. The difficulties? They will be seen as the bearers of hidden resources. And the crises? They will become nothing more to us than the moment to begin!

13

A PILGRIM PROGRESSING

John 16:31–33

IT WAS MY GOOD FORTUNE recently to see a production by the Everyman Players that was based on John Bunyan's classic, *Pilgrim's Progress*. This particular work is much more than an aesthetic exercise. It constitutes an important part of our heritage in the English-speaking world, and its influence is second only to the Bible itself in forming the religious consciousness of the last three hundred years. I would even venture to say that in our culture it is almost impossible to come to terms with the forces that have made us what we are religiously without some awareness of *Pilgrim's Progress*.

In my judgment, this work gives us a realistic image of what the Christian life is really like. It tells us what to expect as we answer the call to follow Christ down the road of life. The very title itself holds the secret, for in the two words, *pilgrim* and *progress*, you have a subtle blending of the struggle and hope which are the essence of the Christian way. It is not just struggle without hope—that would be fatalism. But neither is it hope without struggle—that would be fairyland fantasy. No, John Bunyan saw very clearly that both of these realities constitute the Christian life, and so he gave us an unforgettable image—a pilgrim, a venturer, a struggler, setting out with a pack on his back from one place toward another and, through many struggles, progressing to fulfillment.

Christian—as the hero of *Pilgrim's Progress* is called— was not translated instantly from the City of Destruction to the Celestial City. If you have ever read the work, you know that he journeys for some three hundred pages through all kinds of places and encounters a great variety of obstacles. He gets bogged down in the Slough of Despond, becomes lost in Bypass Meadow, sojourns for a while in places like Doubting Castle and Vanity Fair. And who can forget the characters he meets along the way, like Mr. Worldly-Wise, Helpful, Pliant, Ignorance, and all the rest? By no stretch of the imagination does our hero ride a kind of escalator that automatically lifts him higher. No, he falls down and he gets up repeatedly. He loses his way and has to find it again and again. He experiences moments of real exhilaration and then prolonged periods of depression and despair.

What I am saying is that this image of a pilgrim progressing or a struggler moving forward in hope is the best image I know to describe what it is like to be a Christian in this kind of world. And the gift of such an image can be exceedingly helpful to us right now as we seek to make up our lives amid the complexities of the twentieth century.

For one thing, it can protect us from being disillusioned about the Christian way. More often than not, disillusionment is the child of illusion. If a person has wrong expectations at the outset, he or she is almost certain to be disappointed by actual experience. I think this is what lies behind so much of the negativism and despair we see

in religious circles today. For many, the Christian life has
not turned out the way they thought it would. They tried
it, and they did not like it—and this was not because of
what it was in itself, but because of false expectations that
had been constructed ahead of time. Here is a place
where something like *Pilgrim's Progress* can really be of
help to us.

I will be honest with you—I wish I had come in contact
with this document twenty years earlier than I did. The
spiritual atmosphere in which I was raised was not one
that emphasized hopeful struggle or struggle rooted in
hope; it was rather a highly evangelistic approach which
centered on winning the lost to Christ and getting people
to join the church. What happened was what can happen
with any "super-sales" approach; the tendency was to
"accentuate the positive and eliminate the negative." The
plan of salvation got reduced to a cut-rate price, and in
order to get people in, the church overpromised what life
with Christ was really like. They made it sound like all
hope and no struggle at all.

In fact, to my childish ears, the words, "Christ is the
answer," did not mean that Jesus Christ would come
alongside me and become a gracious Resource and Companion in the struggles of life; I heard those words to
mean that Christ would deliver me *out* of the struggle altogether and give me total peace right then and there
forever. I honestly thought this meant an exact answer to
every question, specific guidance for every dilemma, and
a shield from all misfortunes that befell the other people
outside his grace.

This is the image of the Christian life I formed from the
sermons, the testimonies, and particularly the music I
heard as a child. I remember that, whenever we would
have a service where people could select their favorite
hymns, someone would always call for "The Haven of
Rest," and all would sing:

I have anchored my soul in the haven of rest,
I will sail the wild seas no more;
The tempest may sweep over the wide, stormy deep,
In Jesus I'm safe evermore.

Let me add that it was not just the "lowbrow" gospel hymns that gave such a one-sided view of things. Even a majestic piece like Frederick Faber's "There's a Wideness in God's Mercy" has a last stanza that leaves the same impression:

If our love were but more simple,
We should take him at his word;
And our lives would be all sunshine
In the sweetness of our Lord.

Under the impact of words like these, how could one help but get the impression that Christ delivers us *out* of the struggles of everyday life rather than being our Resource within them?

This one misconception led me through a great deal of pain. At first I bought what my church was selling, as any trusting child would, but it did not work out the way it was advertised. God knows I tried to *make* it work—as earnestly as any adolescent could. I rededicated my life more times than I can number and tried again and again with all earnestness to "let Jesus come into my heart." But even after all this I continued to experience struggles. There were still doubts crowding into my mind crying out for answers. There were many agonizing dilemmas about what I was to do with my life and how to handle my sexual energy and my money, and no neat solutions dropped from the sky or out of the Bible as I had been promised. For a while, I almost gave up on the Christian faith, the way a dissatisfied customer reacts when he has believed an advertisment and been disappointed.

I repeat, I would have been better off to have "cut my

124

spiritual eyeteeth" on *Pilgrim's Progress* rather than on evangelical pietism, for the image Bunyan gives of the Christian life is much more realistic. The disillusionment I had to work through was not really the fault of the Christian gospel. It grew out of the illusion I had been given that Christ saves us *from* struggles rather than through them.

However, the grace of God is both wise and ingenious, and, like Christian in *Pilgrim's Progress,* I was not left to languish in error. It was my good fortune to meet some people who had a different understanding of how "Christ is the answer." Through them I began to see the Christian way in new terms—the way John Bunyan depicts it.

I came to realize that Christ never promised to deliver us from struggle and agony and conflict. Jesus says plainly in John 16:33, "In the world you have tribulation; but be of good cheer, I have overcome the world." And Jesus' own experience of life was a parable of struggle in hope. The very things we read about Christian's experiencing between the City of Destruction and the Celestial City are what Jesus faced during his days and his nights on earth. Therefore, we must not expect him to rescue us out of trouble or to lift us up above the agonies of life. He is not so much above us or beneath us as beside us and within us. He is our Savior in terms of resource and companionship. He gives us courage and insight and hope to keep on facing life and its challenges rather than turning and running away in defeat. Christ does not promise us "a rose garden." He says rather that he has already run this same course, already fought his way through victoriously, and that, with him, we can do the same thing in our own lives. "Lo, I am with you always, even unto the end of the world," he says (Matt. 28:20, KJV). "I have overcome the world, and I will help you do the same."

This is the heroic image Bunyan gives us in *Pilgrim's*

Progress, and believe me, friend, this one works! When we stop expecting rescue and open up to resource, not only does Jesus Christ come alive as our Companion; the whole Bible also takes on new life! No longer is it an abstract book about far-off people; it now becomes "the communion of the saints," "a cloud of witnesses"—the story of people who, like ourselves, had to struggle, and who can teach us something from their lives that can strengthen us for our own coping. I realize now that as a child I did not regard the stories of the Bible in a human, helpful sense. Its heroes were always depicted to me as so grand and perfect that I felt no kinship at all with them. I was fascinated by their exploits, but it never occurred to me to look on them as fellow strugglers and thus resources for my own struggles. It was not until I learned to humanize these heroes and to see them the way the Bible depicts them that they became helpful companions.

Some time ago I heard Keith Miller, an extraordinarily helpful twentieth-century Christian, make this very point. He was underlying the fact that the Christian life is not easy and that all people experience fear and sometimes fall down as they try to follow God's will. Miller said that the story of the Bible is not the account of supermen doing heroic things out of abnormal resources, but rather a story of chicken-hearted folk like you and me who did not give up when they failed, who somehow "kept on keeping on" and dared to put the keys of their future into the hands of a merciful God even when they were afraid.

The people in the Bible struggled along imperfectly, the way Christian struggles in *Pilgrim's Progress*. For example, take Abraham, called "the father of us all," the one who dared venture forth in a time when no individual had ever left his clan to journey by himself. Abraham had nothing more substantial than a sense of promise beckoning him to another land, yet he willingly left the security of the known to venture toward an unspecified destination. Abraham is the one who trusted God enough to take his only son, the fruit of his latter years, and willingly climb a mountain to offer the boy back to God. No wonder such a one is lionized in the Bible! Yet the same document makes clear that, for all his heroism, Abraham was not always a perfect believer. In his movement from the City of Destruction to his own place of promise, Abraham, like all of us, fell down from time to time; he sometimes lost his way; he even stopped trusting in God and began to depend on himself and his own wits.

Once when there was a famine in Palestine, Abraham got scared and forgot all about God's promise to provide. Unbidden, he rushed down to Egypt where food was more plentiful, and in his fright made an incredible proposal to Sarah, his wife. It appears he had shrewdly sized up the situation, and if I may translate the conversation colloquially, he said, "Sarah, I understand the Pharoah down here is quite a lady's man, and you, my dear, are an exceedingly attractive woman. Now listen, if the Pharoah sees you and takes a shine to you, would you do me a favor? Would you tell him that you are my sister and go along with him?" Now this is not exactly the kind of behavior you would expect from the Old Testament's number-one spiritual hero. But the point is that *Abraham was not perfect.* He had to struggle along, falling down and getting up, just like we do. And if we will humanize him and let him come alongside us instead of being way above us, he can be of help. He becomes part of that "band of brothers," that "communion of the saints" that Jesus brings with him to accompany us down the road of life.

What is true of Abraham is true of all the biblical heroes. Was Moses always strong and brave and courageous? The answer, of course, is no. He had his moments of panic, such as after he killed the Egyptian overlord and expected to start a revolution among the Hebrews and nothing happened. He ran like a jackrabbit for the border and hid out for forty years as a herdsman. Then when God called him to go back and set his people free, he had all kinds of misgivings and excuses. You see, Moses was not always "Mr. Strong"—no one is! Why, even Jesus himself got "cold feet" in the Garden of Gethsemane. Three times he tried to get out of the Crucifixion. At that moment he was so tense that he was sweating enough to burst a blood vessel. And of course the outcome was not rescue from the struggle, but resource in the struggle to see it through.

What I am saying is that the Bible has really come alive to me—as has Jesus Christ himself—once I stopped expecting the wrong thing and started accepting what the Christian faith does have to give—courage and companionship and resources in the struggle of life. And this is what I have found in reading *Pilgrim's Progress*. Bunyan's image of a pilgrim progressing against great odds—of a struggler moving forward in hope—can do much to help us all in understanding the Christian way. It is a corrective to the kind of disillusionment to which many of us, because of our backgrounds, have been vulnerable. We of all people need the heroic image of the Christian life which *Pilgrim's Progress* depicts. In fact, I believe this image could become the beginning of a new stage of faith for many of us. I sense great fatigue and exhaustion of spirit in our whole country just now. We have been emptied out by the turmoil of the sixties and the cynicism of the seventies and the renewed threats of nuclear war and economic collapse in the eighties. We are really in need of a transfusion of new life and courage and perspective.

And who knows, perhaps the One who is keenly aware of who we are and where we are just now has provided this old, old story to prepare us for today and tomorrow and the decades to come. It could do for you now what it first did for me twenty years ago; it could open up a new perspective on the Christian life as one of both struggle and hope, not just one or the other. Perhaps Jesus Christ will emerge for you as who he really is—a resource in the midst of conflict, not a rescue from the conflict itself; a very present help in time of trouble, not a deliverer out of the trouble. And perhaps this new understanding of Christ will also make real to you "the communion of the saints" that is the Bible. What we have here is not the account of what God can do with angels, but the story of what he can do with ordinary, frightened, sinful human beings like ourselves who did not give up but had the courage to keep on. We must never forget that today's legendary achievements—awesome as they may seem—were yesterday's risky adventures. Courage is not the capacity never to be afraid; as Karl Barth reminds us, "Courage is fear that has said its prayers." This is what biblical heroes, rightly understood, can teach us. The Savior who comes alongside as a resource brings with him a band of brothers to be our companions on the way, and this is the kind of experience *Pilgrim's Progress* opened up for me.

Here is a fine image of what the Christian life is all about. A pilgrim negotiating challenges, one after another, but in it all progressing, moving forward in hope. I hope we can see in Christian a reflection of our own identity and resolve to do with our days and nights here on earth what he did. What was that? In Bunyan's own words, every time Christian found himself face to face with a problem, "he considered that he had no armor for his back. . . . Therefore, he resolved to venture and move forward. And so he went on!" May God grant us the vision through this experience to go and do likewise.

14

TO WALK AND NOT TO FAINT

Isaiah 40:27–31

IN MY JUDGMENT one of the most perceptive Christian writers of the twentieth century was C. S. Lewis, the brilliant professor of Medieval English Literature at Oxford and Cambridge. Lewis remained a bachelor until his late fifties and then married another adult convert to the Christian faith, Joy Davidman. At the time of their marriage, Miss Davidman was suffering from cancer. She experienced a brief remission, which brought them both a period of great joy, but then she relapsed, and his bride of only a few years slowly died away before his eyes.

Soon after his wife's funeral, Lewis began to jot down some of his thoughts in the back of old notebooks, and just before his own death these were put together and published in a little book entitled *A Grief Observed*. It is one of the most poignant documents of its kind I have ever read. At the beginning of the book, Lewis makes no effort to hide his profound disappointment in his religion. What has occurred in the depths of his grief was not at all what he had expected. The early pages literally reek with a disillusionment that borders on despair. However, as he continues to work through the grief process, Lewis begins to realize that the problem may not have been so much with God as with himself. It was his expectations, not the experiences themselves, that lay at the heart of the problem. He discovers what is often the secret of disillusionment; namely, that it is the offspring of illusion.

Many times we experience disappointment because we have started out with the wrong kinds of expectations. Either out of our own imaginations or from what others have told us, we anticipate what future experience is going to be like. Then when we arrive at the moment itself, we find the reality to be something quite different indeed. The actual is almost always iconoclastic to our expectations. Rarely, if ever, does what happens prove to be identical to what we have anticipated. It is moving indeed to watch Lewis in these pages gradually gain distance and perspective on his bereavement and come to an entirely different evaluation of what his religion had meant to him in the depth of crisis. The little book ends on a much brighter note than marks its beginning.

I had occasion to remember this experience some years ago when a close friend of mine asked me abruptly, "Does God really help a person in time of trouble?" At that moment, I myself was coming out of one of the most trying experiences of my whole existence. Some nine months before this time, my little daughter had been diagnosed with acute leukemia, but very quickly she had been given a medicine that enabled her to go into a remission, and for some time she had been almost perfectly normal. Naturally, this had created many distant hopes in my mind. Had the diagnosis been a mistaken one? Had she experienced the miracle of divine healing that I and so many others had prayed for?

At any rate, all of these hopes had come to an abrupt end, ironically, on Easter Sunday morning, when the old pains reappeared and she went into a severe relapse that involved hospitalization for some two weeks. Part of the time both of her eyes were swollen shut, and pain racked every part of her body. Moving with her through those two weeks was an unspeakably draining experience. I found myself stretched in every way—physically exhausted, emotionally dissipated, my faith itself challenged as never before.

The worst moment of all for me came one night when my daughter could get no relief, and she asked me, "When will this leukemia go away?" I answered, "I don't know, darling, but we are doing everything in our power to find an answer to cure it." There was a long silence, and then she asked in the darkness, "Have you asked God when the leukemia will go away?" I hedged a bit and said, "You know, darling, how we have prayed again and again for God to help us." But she persisted: "Have you asked God when it will go away? What did he say?" And I simply put the question to you—how do you respond to such childlike directness at a time when the heavens seem utterly silent and even locked from the inside?

My point is, I was utterly exhausted by the time we finally located another medicine and were able to get her some relief, and it was just at this moment that my friend thrust his question before me. He knew where I had been and what I was going through, which of course was why he was making such an inquiry. He was full of intensity as he looked me in the eye and said, "Give it to me straight. I am not asking you this as a preacher. I am asking you as an honest human being. Was there Anybody or Anything down there at the bottom? When the chips were really down, does this 'thing' we call God really make any difference?"

He was too good a friend, and the situation was far too serious for me to attempt to put up a front or to trot out a pat answer. The only thing appropriate for that moment was honest reporting. I thought for a long time, and then said quietly, "Yes, I can honestly say there was Something down there in the darkness. The mystery of Godness was present. I was given help. But let me be very specific. It was a special kind of help. It was not the sort of thing I have heard other people talk about when they were in deep circumstances, and yet, for me, it was very real." Then I went on to share with him how I had been helped by the famous promise in Isaiah 40 that "they who wait for the Lord shall renew their strength, they shall mount up with wings like eagles, they shall run and not be weary, they shall walk and not faint (v.31). We discussed the matter at length, for I remembered C. S. Lewis's experience of disappointment. In speaking of hope, I did not want to overpromise and thus set my friend up for disillusionment.

What does this particular scripture say to us? Verse 31 begins with the very specific promise: "They who wait for the Lord shall renew their strength." The author here is talking about people who take God seriously, who open their lives to him; to "wait for the Lord" is to look to him and to depend upon him. To these kind of folk a specific promise is made—they will be given strength from Beyond. They will experience an increase of energy, a supplement of power not theirs before. However, on the heels of this specific promise, the writer goes on to describe three different ways in which this strength of God can come to people. In my judgment, these distinctions are crucial, for they will safeguard us against what happened to Lewis—expecting one thing and then experiencing something very different. Let us note carefully the variety of religious experiences that the writer here specifies.

First, he speaks of ecstasy—the experience of "rising up with wings as eagles." Here is an utterly authentic way for the life of God to come into our lives, and the experience of such moments of exuberance and abandon and celebration has always been a part of biblical religion. There is a hint from the very beginning that this is part of the nature of God himself. Do you recall how one of the Genesis accounts depicts God as looking out over all he had been creating and finding it "very good"? He promptly proceeded to take a day off simply to celebrate the wonder of "isness." This is ecstasy. To be caught up out of one's self in joy over some reality is exactly the sort of experience God wants each one of us to have, for remember we are made in his image, and to look like and be like our "Daddy" is our true destiny. Right here is where much of the creativity of life is to be found—when we let "the child within us" out to play and to leap and to celebrate.

King David was not above this kind of exuberance. When the Ark of the Covenant was retrieved from captivity among the Philistines and at long last was brought back into the Holy City, David was so jubilant over this event that he danced himself into a frenzy. In fact, it is even implied that he danced right out of his clothes! His wife, Michal, was a much more controlled and sedate sort, and she was repelled by David's show of religious enthusiasm. When he came home that night she rebuked him stingingly for having made a spectacle of himself before the people. "It was beneath the good taste of a king," she sniffed.

It is interesting to note that this Michal, who abhorred ecstasy, remained barren all of her life. She never bore any children for the king, and I think there is a direct connection between this incapacity for ecstasy and unfruitfulness. The point I am making is that times of "soaring with wings as eagles" under the impact of God's

Spirit are an utterly valid form of religious experience, and I hope we can cultivate this side of our religion and grow in our ability to celebrate. However, we must realize that this is not the only way God gives his strength to human beings, and woe unto us if we absolutize this form of religious experience and say, "If there is no ecstasy, God is not with us." This is a sure formula for disillusionment, for, believe me, there are certain moments in life, such as when you are standing by the bed of your dying child, when ecstasy not only is impossible; it is totally inappropriate.

The writer goes on to describe a second form that the strength of God can assume, namely, energy for activism: "They shall run and not be weary." Here is another authentic experience of biblical religion—the inspiration to rise to a challenge and to tackle some task that needs to be done. We are all aware of the claim that religion has been an enemy of human progress rather than its instigator. Karl Marx called the Christianity he saw the "opiate of the people," and, sadly enough, at times this has been true. However, there is other evidence that Christianity can be "the thyroid of the spirit"; that is, it can motivate men and women to heroic, problem-solving activity. If you will look into the history of our own country, you will see that almost all the schools and hospitals and other serving institutions were born of religious impulses.

One of the pioneers in the field of American social work was Jane Adams, a wealthy young woman who could not ignore the ravages an industrial and urban society was taking on family life, particularly on children. She was religiously moved to be disturbed about the slums of Chicago, and one day as she mulled over the problem she felt two questions being addressed to her: "If not you, who? If not now, when?" Thus, like the young Isaiah, she was not drafted into humanitarian service; she volunteered: "Here am I, Lord, send me." And by the inspiration of the Father's love, she became a legendary helper in the social work field.

This is an authentic expression of how God affects the human spirit. The energy for activism—the power to "run and not be weary"—is one of the forms that an experience of God can assume. However, once again, this is not the totality of divine experience. It is not the only way that the strength of God can be encountered. For again, there are times when you are standing helpless by the side of a dying child, where there is no room to run, no way for activism to change the situation, and if this is your only understanding of religious experience, it is an illusion that will inevitably lead to disillusionment.

But there is a third part to Isaiah's promise, and that is the gift of endurance—the strength "to walk and not faint." In some ways, this may look like the least of the three forms of divine strength. Some commentators have even questioned the sequence of Isaiah's process. Should not it have been the other way around—endurance the least significant, then energy, and finally the climax of ecstasy? Do we not walk and then run and finally soar as our final consummation in God? If I had never suffered much, I might have accepted such a view. But out of the experience that was mine some years ago, I now recognize that the one who wrote this had a profound understanding of human need. For the truth is that the hardest challenges in life come not at the point of strength, but at the point of helplessness and weakness. What is more difficult, I ask you, than trying "to keep on keeping on" when you find yourself surrounded by immensities you cannot change and when there is nothing to do except hold on and try to endure? When there is no occasion to soar and no place to run, then the promise of strength "to walk and not faint," small as it may seem, becomes infinitely significant and appropriate; in fact, it is the best gift of all.

Josef Pieper has observed that in such moments of weakness, temptation becomes very acute, and that it takes one of two forms—either presumption or despair. For example, when we find ourselves really "up against it," there is the temptation to explode in bitterness, to curse God and circumstances, and to attempt to be more than we are as helpless, finite creatures. But if presumption is not the road we take, despair is the other dark alternative. Simply to give up, to say with a sigh of resignation, "I have had it. I quit. Stop the world; I want to get off"—this is a very real temptation. It is to this situation that the last and climactic form of God's promise of strength comes. When nothing else is possible, the strength to endure, "to walk and not faint," is given— the gift of patience, of just holding on. Mind you, this is not the only way God comes to us, but when you find yourself utterly hemmed in, it becomes the most appropriate way of all.

I looked my friend straight in the eye that day and said that it was in this latter sense that God had helped me in my experience in the darkness. I made clear to him that there had been no ecstasy in those last two weeks. I have read devotional books where it is promised that if we will simply lift up our eyes and turn to God in prayer, all problems will instantly dissolve and every darkness will be caught up in light and we will soar above our difficulties as if they do not exist. There is something in me that wants to cry out to such claims: "Bunk! Those who write this way have never really stood in the darkness or are utterly dishonest in what they report." However, I realize this is a presumptive reaction on my part. All I can say is that, for me, in my place of darkness, this did not happen. There was no ecstasy.

Neither was there an infusion of light or power that gave me conclusive "answers" as to why this was happening or practical suggestions of things that could be done. I still, to this day, do not understand why innocent little children have to suffer. I did my very best for eighteen months to find a solution to leukemia, but was unsuccessful. Thus, there was no experience of "running and not being weary."

Yet I can report honestly that strength "to walk and not faint" was given. No ecstasy. No great energy. Just the gift of endurance—that was all that met me in the depths of darkness. I did not soar with wings or run a step. But, by the grace of God, *somehow I stayed on my feet!* I did not blow up in presumptive bitterness; neither did I give up in hopeless despair. I was given the gift just to stand and hold on. And I honestly doubt I could have done that without the support of the kind of God Isaiah reminds us of in this passage. These descriptive images of him were very significant to me. He is "the Everlasting Lord" and "the Creator of the ends of the earth," which means that at all times and in every place he is present. He is there as Mystery, for his "understanding is unsearchable." Yet, even as Mystery, he is not remote or distant or weary. He is there as the One who "gives power to the faint, and to him who has no might . . . increases strength" (Isa. 40:29). That is his nature, and I can honestly say that again and again, in those endless nights in a hospital room, he came and quietly, faithfully gave "power to the faint" and increased the strength of one "who had no might."

It is in this sense that I could say honestly, "God really does help in time of trouble," and I am not afraid to voice that promise now. Believe me, whoever you are and whatever your circumstances, God can tangibly help you in your trouble, provided you realize the different forms his strength can take, and provided you are willing to accept what he gives rather than what you may desire.

I began this chapter by referring to C. S. Lewis and his initial disappointment in what his religion meant to him in an experience of bereavement. He came to see that the problem was in him, not in God, that false expectations, not divine inadequacy, were the cause of his difficulty. We would do well to remember this. If we decide ahead of time what has to happen and then demand this of reality, we are almost sure to be disappointed. But if we can remember that God has different gifts for different moments in life and that he can be trusted to give us what we need when we need it, then help will become available. A trust in his adequacy and a humility of spirit that is willing to accept what is offered are the keys to receiving what he gives.

Hear, then, the promise: There is help to be had from God. You can count on it. It might take the form of ecstasy, when you "mount up with wings as eagles." It could come in the form of energy, when you "run and are not weary." Or then again, it may be simply the strength to "walk and not faint." This latter may seem like a little thing, but when you are really "up against it," when you have no occasion to soar and no room to run, believe me, it is not. In those moments, the gifts of endurance and patience become utterly important—just to stay on your feet and not give up. And I can say out of honest experience that if you are willing "to wait upon the Lord" and accept this gift, you *will not be disappointed*. You may not be able to soar or even to run, but to walk and not faint—*it will be given!*

And there are times, my friend, when that not only is enough; it is everything.

15

GRATITUDE IS A CHOICE

Genesis 37:50

ONE SUMMER ON VACATION I was browsing through a book shop when my eye was caught by an intriguing title. The little paperback was called *The Choice Is Always Ours*. I picked it up, and it turned out to be an anthology of religious writings around the central theme that in every given situation we humans do have alternatives. The book makes it very clear that we are not free to determine what happens to us in terms of objective events. Many forces over which we have no control converge on our lives. What we are free to do is determine how we will respond to these events.

The book also acknowledges that such choices are rarely simple or clear-cut. Life as most of us experience it is not one thing but many; that is, what we face in a given situation is not all light or all darkness, total goodness or total evil, but a baffling mixture of light *and* darkness, goodness *and* evil, factors that are going for us *and* factors that are going against us. Our human freedom therefore, is usually exercised in a context of ambiguity. This makes all the more important the reality that will be the thrust of this chapter—the thing called thanksgiving or gratitude. It is going to be my contention in this chapter that gratitude, more than anything else, is the difference between just "making the best" of life and making the *most* of it.

You see, in every given situation, the choice that is always ours is this: We can ask the resentment question—"Why did this have to happen to me?"—and concentrate on the negative, on what is going against us. Or we can ask the gratitude question—"What is there here to be thankful for that can be used in constructing a positive future?"—and then focus in on that which is going for us. Obviously, these are two very different ways of approaching a single event, and I would like to suggest that one leads to victorious and courageous living while the other leads to immobilization and despair.

Let me confess that I have not always had such a high view of thankfulness. Like all children from my background, I was carefully taught the discipline of gratitude from the first. I knew I was supposed to say "thank you" when anything nice was done for me, and this even went so far as having to put it down on paper. As a young boy, I always used to have a "let down" feeling on December 26, and part of that heaviness was due to the prospect of having to sit down and write those interminable "thank you" notes to assorted aunts and uncles and cousins.

The point is that initially I thought of gratitiude in terms of burden and obligation. It was one of those things that was demanded of me. It was only after I grew older and began to be influenced by Holy Scriptures that I came to feel differently about this reality. I now see it as a resource rather than a burden. The practice of learning to look thankfully at a given situation is far more than a social obligation. It is a way of getting in touch with what you have going for you amid all that is going against you, and thus is a source of creative energy that enables us to overcome obstacles rather than to be overcome by them. I cannot say too much about the functional value of gratitude when it comes to what Charles Boddie calls "copeability." Thankfulness is a potent resource for living, and there is no one in all the world who has taught me this lesson better than the Old Testament character Joseph.

Many of you will remember that this Joseph's early childhood was somewhat unusual. He was the first-born son of the woman his father had loved from the first time he laid eyes upon her. Jacob had worked and waited for fourteen years to make Rachel his wife, and then for a long time she had been unable to bear children. When she finally did conceive and Joseph was born, predictably he was surrounded by inordinate attention. By that time Jacob had ten other sons, but none received from their father what Joseph did. He had more given to him and less asked of him than all the rest, and that celebrated coat of his became a symbol of the unhealthy inequity in the family. The King James Version calls this coat "a coat of many colors," but a more accurate translation of the Hebrew would be "a long coat with sleeves." This was obviously not the kind of garment that one could work in, but the sort of thing a person of leisure would wear around the house. Little Joseph grew up in a sheltered world of preference and privilege, and it is not surprising that he became spoiled and arrogant—as the dreams he began having clearly indicated.

When Joseph was seventeen years old, Jacob did something that revealed just how insensitive he was to the feelings of the rest of his sons. He had the audacity to send the idle Joseph—all dressed up in his leisure coat— out to see how the working brothers were doing in the fields! You can imagine what an explosion of hostility this set off. When "the unblessed sons" saw their father's pet coming through the fields, away from Jacob's protecting hand, all their pent-up frustrations erupted, and for a moment it looked as if they were going to tear Joseph limb from limb with their bare hands. What a shock this hostility must have been to the sheltered Joseph! This was a boy who had never been allowed to see the harsh and violent side of life, and I am sure he was thoroughly traumatized when Reuben stepped in and suggested that his brothers think things over before they went so far as shedding the blood of their own kinsman. Joseph was temporarily confined in a well that was dry at the time, and the Scriptures say that his brothers casually proceeded to eat their lunch as they deliberated on what to do with this human life.

In all probability, Joseph overheard these conversations, and what a revelation it must have been for him to discover what the "real" world was actually like! This human existence of ours is not all sweetness and light. There are callous and cruel individuals who are willing to shed blood and lie to their fathers and do all sorts of atrocious things. That time in the well may not have been very long in terms of actual hours, but it represented "light years" in the maturing of the young Joseph. He was forced to learn in a hurry that this world of ours is not one thing but many, and that one has to develop some strategy for coping with such ambiguity. From the way he responded later on, it appears that Joseph really did "come of age" that day down in the well. He might well have been killed had not some Midianite traders come by at that moment and Reuben hit on an idea that would rid the family of Joseph without going to the extreme of blood-guilt. He persuaded his brothers to sell their brother to these traders, and so off Joseph went toward the land of Egypt and away from Palestine.

Now the miracle to me is that Joseph did not collapse completely at this junction. How easy it would have been for such a trauma to have wiped out this one who had never known hardship before. Why did it not? I believe it was because somehow, back in that well, as he "came of age" about the nature of the real world, Joseph also "came of age" as to how to cope creatively with ambiguity. He began to practice what I call "the strategy of gratitude." That is, instead of saying, "Why is all this happening to me?" and exploding in resentment, he asked rather, "What is there to be thankful for in this situation? What is there among these broken pieces that I can use in building for the future?" When the issue was looked at that way, it was easy to see that there was an occasion for gratitude. After all, had it not been for the intervention of Rueben and the coincidence of the traders coming by when they did, Joseph's life might well have been over. To be sure, he did not have much at that moment, walking along as a slave, the property of someone else headed to a foreign land. He certainly did not have what he once had back in the favor and luxury of his father's house. But he did have his life! He was alive and well in history, and I believe Joseph chose to concentrate on and to make the most of that fact rather than all the negatives in his situation.

That is what I mean by gratitude making the difference amid the ambiguities of life. In every situation, we all have a choice as to what we will maximize and what we will minimize, and the person who has learned to evaluate situations in terms of gratitude rather than despair is far better equipped than all others to cope. This is the way Joseph chose to handle life, and again and again it enabled him in the worst of times to do the best of things.

For example, when the Midianites got to Egypt they sold him to a man named Potiphar. That word in Hebrew means "the one whom God gives," and I think it is the Scripture writer's subtle way of describing how Joseph chose to feel about his new master. Realize now, Joseph could have been filled with resentment at being placed under the absolute authority of any person. After all, he had been utterly free to do as he pleased up to this point in his life. Yet instead of concentrating on that, he chose to be grateful for the kind of man who had bought him, for Potiphar turned out to be not just any slave owner; he was a humane and discerning man who quickly realized that this young foreigner was far above average. The "one whom God had given" to Joseph at this moment gave him a chance to prove himself, and as a result Joseph developed in ways he never would have under the pampering of his father. Choosing to be grateful rather than resentful enabled Joseph to make the most of his working situation, and before long he had risen to the place of overseer of all Potiphar's household.

But being sold into slavery did not end the tests to which Joseph was put. After he had made a place for himself in Potiphar's household, the wife of the house became attracted to the handsome young Hebrew. When he refused again and again to give in to her seductions, she reversed the facts on him and accused Joseph of having done to her what she had done to him. When she told this story to her husband, Potiphar was understandably infuriated. He had Joseph put into the royal prison, where once again the young man's spirit was tried to the limit.

How easy it would have been at that point to give way to bitterness and say, "What kind of world is this where, when you try to do right, things still go wrong?" The temptation to resentment must have been overwhelming, but I believe that once again Joseph chose to take the approach of gratitude. Instead of harboring resentment he proceeded to ask, "What is there here to be thankful for?"

And once again he found something! He said to himself, "You know, I am lucky to be alive. Most slaves, accused as I was, would have been executed on the spot."

Here, as back in the Midianite caravan, Joseph did not have much. There was rampant injustice in what had happened to him, and he had nothing facing him except prison, but at least he was alive and had access to some kind of future. I believe the strategy of gratitude is what kept Joseph from "blowing up" or "giving up"; it was the secret of his incredible resilience. For finally, as you know, Joseph's fortunes did turn and the seemingly impossible occurred. Because of his faithfulness and ingenuity as a servant in the prison, he came to the attention of the Pharaoh at a critical moment in the life of the kingdom. His ability to interpret dreams and offer counsel was so impressive that the Pharaoh in one fell swoop put him in complete charge of all Egypt.

Seventeen years after he had been brought into the country as a foreign slave, Joseph emerged in a position second only to that of the Pharaoh. His story is an incredible illustration of how the providence of God works; here is a God who can take actions that are born of nothing but evil—like what the brothers did out of jealousy or what Potiphar's wife did out of lust—and still work them around for good. But Joseph's story also illustrates another important truth—the difference gratitude can make when it comes to coping with difficult and ambiguous situations.

We humans do have a choice in the great drama of experience. We are not free to determine what happens to us, but we *are* free to determine what response we will make to events. One alternative is the way of resentment; we can focus in on the bad and ask angrily, "Why did this have to happen?" The other alternative is the way of gratitude; this involves sifting through an event and asking, "What is there here to be thankful for? Amid all this

THE LIGHT WITHIN YOU

wreckage, what can I use to build toward the future?"

This is the choice that is always ours, and it is my contention that it is the second alternative—gratitude—that makes the crucial difference between being a victim of or a victor over events. Where does a person get the courage in the worst of times to keep on doing the best of things? By learning to evaluate events from the perspective of gratitude rather than resentment.

This is what our Pilgrim forefathers did back in 1621. You have heard many times how that little band of Puritans set out on the Mayflower for Virginia, only to get blown off course and finally come to shore along Cape Cod. The winter was much worse than they anticipated, and by April only fifty of the original one hundred two had survived. A serious discussion arose as to whether those remaining should give up and go back to the Old World, but they finally decided to stay on and plant a few acres of corn and barley. When the time of the first anniversary of their landing rolled around, discussion arose as to how it should be observed. Some proposed a day of mourning, when attention would be focused on all those who lay in unmarked graves in foreign soil. The others said, "No, a day of thanksgiving would be more appropriate. After all, fifty of us have survived. We have gathered in a good harvest. The Indians have been our friends. Let's focus on what we have going for us, not on what we have going against us." And it just could be that that was the turning point in the founding of this country! Had those Pilgrims chosen to mourn rather than give thanks, would they have found the courage to hold out as they did?

That is a question of history I have no way of answering for certain, but of this I am sure: Of all the forces that enable one to cope with life, gratitude is the most potent. Look at what this approach to life did for Joseph. Look at what it did for the Pilgrims. And think of what it could do for you. So, the next time you are up against the difficulties of life—shattered by the unexpected or the catastrophic—I challenge you: Instead of asking, "Why has this happened to me?" ask rather, "What is there here to be thankful for?" This is the way to power, to courage, to victory.

The choice is always ours! May God grant that it be gratitude!

16

DO YOU REALLY WANT TO GROW?

Mark 1:1–8

DOWN THROUGH THE YEARS, as the church has sought to prepare for the coming of Christ in the Advent season, John the Baptist has been an exceedingly important figure, and for good reason. He is the one, you will remember, who actually prepared the way for Christ's coming in the first century. He was the forerunner, the "advance man," the long expected "Elijah" who would set the stage for the ministry of Jesus. Had it not been for the work of John, Jesus could not have accomplished what he did. Therefore, it is natural that each year the church should look seriously at John's preparatory work and ask, "What is there here that might help us get ready for the coming of Christ?"

In order to answer this, we need to get in mind exactly what John did. It is clear from all four of the Gospel records that John created quite a stir before Jesus ever appeared on the scene. There in the Judean wilderness, where he had grown up, John began to preach with a

strange and compelling power. In the fortieth chapter of
Isaiah, God had commanded that prophet to "speak
home to the hearts of Jerusalem," and this is exactly what
John the Baptist did. His words were charged with power
and vitality. They were able somehow to penetrate
deeper than just the ear and the mind. They got down to
the heart, to that region where people feel and deliberate
and act. And at that level John was able to accomplish a
most delicate feat; he managed to kindle in his followers
the desire to grow and change, even in spite of the natural human tendency to resist such an impulse.

There is in most of us a deep ambivalence about
change. On the one hand, there is much in us that wants
to grow and expand and develop. Human beings are not
by nature static creatures who find joy in immobility. The
instinct for adventure and becoming is a part of our very
beings, and the prospect of the new excites us. At the
same time, there are other parts of us that recoil in resistance before the prospect of change. Our fears are acti-
vated—what will the not-yet-experienced be like? Our
pride and shame are called forth, especially if someone
demands we change or suggests that we should change
because we are "not OK" as we are. And then there is
that weary inertia that simply does not want to make the
effort to undergo and adjust to all that change entails.
This is the inner challenge a call to grow always faces—
which is why John's ministry was so remarkable. He was
able to cut through all this ambivalence and to mobilize
the positive against the negative. This is what was happening to all these people who came from Jerusalem and
Judea and across the Jordan to hear him and then be baptized. The success of John's ministry represented the victory of growth over fear, progress over inertia. John was
able to set life in motion again, and this is always the
preparation that leads up to something great. The desire
for growth must be rekindled if change is to come.

This is precisely what the act of baptism is all about. It was never meant to signal the end of a process. Baptism has always been a symbolic way of saying, "I am ready to grow. Just as once I came out of the watery womb and stood ready to develop in a larger world, so now again I feel the surge of new life and willingly entrust myself to God's creative power to grow me beyond where I am." This is precisely the frame of mind John was able to evoke in people, which is why he baptized and why he came to be identified with this particular act. He was able "to speak home to the hearts" of people—to "get to" them where it really counts, and call forth in them the most important single reality in the human equation—a desire to grow.

When you stop and think about it, this is the one thing we humans bring to the process of creation. We did not call ourselves into being, or have any "say-so" about the potential that is within us. That vast pressure toward maturity which courses throughout all creation is not of our making; it is of God. The only thing we can bring to this process is our willingness or unwillingness. We are so made that we can choose either to flow with the universe and grow toward God's dream for us or to set ourselves against the tide and refuse to move. This is why the element of desire is so important. If it is present, then literally all things are possible under God. If it is not, then not even an omnipotent God is willing to force it to be.

I once read in a marriage counseling manual that the most important single ingredient in a successful marriage is the desire to make it work. The author said that if this reality is present in both parties, there is hardly any conceivable difficulty that they can not find a way to overcome. However, if such a desire is not present, no amount of favorable circumstances can guarantee the success of the marriage. I would agree with this, and I also

153

believe that principle can be extended to all of life. If we really want to grow and change and are willing to pay the price involved, there is no end to what we can become: "Eye hath not seen, nor ear heard, neither have entered into the heart of man, the things which God hath prepared for them that love him" (1 Cor. 2:9, KJV). But if that desire does not exist, because it has been choked out by fear or pride or shame or inertia or whatever, not even the God who made heaven and earth has the power to make us be what we were created to be.

This is exactly the point Jesus made the day he walked beside the Pool of Bethesda, where so many sick people gathered. There was a tradition in that place that when the waters stirred an angel was nearby, and the first person to get into the pool would be healed of his affliction. Thus, from all around, the blind and the lame and the mute gathered near the pool in hope of healing. As Jesus moved through this assembly of agony, his attention was drawn to one particularly pathetic man who had been lying there for thirty-eight years. Jesus went up to him and asked simply, "Do you want to be healed?"

On the surface, that sounds like a ridiculous question. Does not everyone want to be well? Why would this man have waited so long if he had not wanted to be healed? Yet Jesus was aware of what we have already mentioned—that the process of change is never simple. And sure enough, the man's response reflected ambivalence. He began to make excuses and shift the blame to other people. "The problem is," he said, "I have no one to help me into the pool, and when the water bubbles, someone else always gets in ahead of me."

But Jesus would not let him evade the issue. He persisted: "I want to know—do *you* want to be healed? This is the real issue. Have you become so accustomed to this life of dependency that you really do not want to change? After all, there are benefits as well as drawbacks to being an invalid. No one expects anything of you. You do not have to work. You do not face the pressure active people face. And would you really accept help if it were offered? It takes a unique form of strength to acknowledge need and to accept assistance from another. You have to swallow pride and shame and a sense of self-sufficiency. What I am asking you is the real question—right here, right now, do you want to be healed?" For the first time probably in thirty-eight years, the real issue was spelled out for this man. He could no longer evade or blame. Did he or did he not want to change?

This is the question it always comes back to—the question of desire. Confronting that question is what always goes before any significant event of growth. And when the paralytic by the Pool of Bethesda was confronted with that question, he dared to answer, "Yes, with all that this entails, I want to change." Then immediately the process of healing began. A thirty-eight-year cycle was broken, and a new way of living began to take shape. Power this man did not know he possessed began to flow, and he began to take responsibility for carrying his own load rather than being carried. To be sure, there were pains in this new way of life; significant change is always an experience of both gain and loss. But look at the new possibilities that were available to this man! He had a whole new world before him once he made the decision to grow, and such is the case for anyone who is willing to venture forth. It is never too late to start growing again, no matter how old we are. If after thirty-eight years of immobility this man could begin to move again, why not each of us?

Here, then, is undoubtedly why year after year the church turns back to John the Baptist to help get ready for Christmas. Before any significant new thing can occur in life, there has to be a rebirth of the desire to grow. John was able to accomplish this by making people feel simultaneously dissatisfied with the way they were and hopeful of what they could be. Both aspects are necessary if a wholesome desire to grow is to be born. Without some sense of need and a recognition that change ought to take place, there would be no impetus to grow. But without the hope that something can be done, repentance would only lead to despair. This was John's genius—he was both harsh and hopeful. He demanded "fruits worthy of repentance," and yet at the same time pointed toward the coming of a Resource who would baptize with the Holy Spirit and shed the love of God abroad in human hearts. In this way, he accomplished the classic work of preparation; he mobilized the positive desire to grow against the negative forces of resistance, which is another way of saying he set the stage for the fire of creativity to be lit all over again.

And what could be more appropriate just now than having John revisit us to "speak home to our hearts" and rekindle in us the desire to grow? No one could ever do a more important thing for us than setting the issue squarely before us. Do you want to be healed? Do you want to grow? Do you want to be different? This is the question on which everything turns, and it is by no means a simple matter. The process of growth involves promise and enlargement and excitement, but it also entails letting go and feeling uncertainty and having to adapt to the new. Make no mistake about it, growth is always gain and loss, but the two are not equal. What one gets on the way of venturing with God is always more than what one loses. But every person has to decide for himself or herself how much or how little he or she will settle for.

The tragedy of life, I believe, can assume one of two forms. One can be arrogant and try to take more of life than is possible. The Greek called this "hubris"; it was the sin of Prometheus and Hitler. But far more common, I think, is the tragedy at the other end of this spectrum, namely, settling for too little, not aspiring enough and thus "falling short" of the glory that could be. I have always been moved by the story of a little boy around the turn of the century who lived far back out in the country. He had reached the age of twelve and had never in all his life seen a circus. Therefore, you can imagine his excitement one day when a poster went up at school that on the next Saturday a traveling circus was coming to the nearby town. He ran home with the glad news, and then came the question, "Daddy, can I go?" The family was poor, but the father sensed how important this was to the lad, so he said, "If you will do your Saturday chores ahead of time, I'll see to it that you have the money to go."

Come Saturday morning the chores were done and the little boy stood dressed in his Sunday best by the breakfast table. His father reached down in his overalls and pulled out a dollar bill—the most money the little boy had ever had at one time in all his life. The father cautioned him to be careful and then sent him on his way to town. He was so excited his feet hardly seemed to touch the ground all the way. As he got on the outskirts of the village, he noticed that people were lining the streets and he worked his way through the crowd until he could see what was coming. And there, lo and behold, in the distance approached the spectacle of a circus parade! It was the grandest thing this lad had ever beheld. There were animals in cages and bands and midgets and all that goes to make up such a phenomenon. Finally after everything had passed where he was standing, the traditional circus clown, with floppy shoes and baggy pants and brightly painted face, came bringing up the rear. As the clown passed where he was standing the little boy reached into his pocket and got out that precious dollar bill. Handing the money to the clown, the boy then turned around and went home.

What had happened? *The boy thought he had seen the cir-*

cus when he had only seen the parade! And somehow I think this illuminates the pathos of so many human lives. The tragedy is not that we arrogantly aspire too high. It is rather that we settle for so little. Here is what we could be, and yet because of fear or ignorance or shame or inertia we take the precious dollars of our lives and settle for the parade rather than the Real Thing.

This brings me back to the point of this whole chapter, which is that the ministry of John the Baptist is an eternal one. What did he do that made it possible for Christ to come? He brought to a head the issue of the desire. He got the people to face openly and positively the question, "Do you want to grow?" Thus, when Jesus came, the ground was broken, the time was fulfilled, the "fields white unto harvest." And if John is to help us just now, this same issue must be raised, the same question asked. Do you want to grow? If you do, then the sky is the limit. God is "able to do exceeding abundantly above all that we ask or think" (Eph. 3:20, KJV). But if not, then not even the power that set the stars in space can fulfill his dream for you. Your desire is absolutely crucial. This is the opening that gives or denies God access to our potential; in the final analysis, it is the hinge of our destiny. In God's eyes, in fact, our desires are more important than our deeds.

I have always been moved by that section of 2 Samuel where King David looked about him at his fine palace and remembered that the Ark of the Convenant was being housed in a tent. Then and there he "got it in his heart" to build a magnificent temple for the Lord. As you know, for many reasons David was never able to complete that project. It was his son Solomon who finally brought that dream into concrete reality. This was a disappointment for David, but one night God said to him, "Don't worry, David, the fact that you had it in your heart to build the temple is enough. What matters to me is that you wanted to."

This is an awesome thought, is it not—that our sincere desires are really what matter in the eyes of God? And yet I think that is true. If the desire to grow and do God's will is present, that is what really matters. The rest can be left in his hands. Our desire is what we bring to the cosmic process. Thomas Merton, the great modern Catholic contemplative, understood this well. During one of the times when he was experiencing deep depression, he wrote this following prayer in his journal: "My Lord God, I have no idea where I am going. I do not see the road ahead of me. I cannot know for certain where it will end. Nor do I really know myself. And the fact that I think I am following your will does not mean that I am actually doing so. But I believe, dear Father, that the desire to please You does in fact please You, and I hope that I have that desire in all that I am doing. I hope that I will never do anything apart from that desire. And so I believe that if I do this, You will lead me by the right road, though I may know nothing about it. Therefore, I will trust You always; though I may seem to be lost in the shadow of death, I will not fear, for You are with me and You will never leave me to face my peril alone."

That is it! The desire to please God is what pleases him. This is why the ministry of John was so significant in the first century and why it continues to have significance every year, even to this very moment. There is nothing more basic in life than the desire to grow. If it is present, no number of obstacles can keep God from finishing that which he has begun. If it is not present, then not even the almighty Creator can make his dream come true.

17

NO RESTING PLACE

1 Kings 3:3–14, 11:4,9

THE BIBLICAL KINSPERSON who is the subject of this chapter has the distinction of being one of the few Old Testament characters to whom Jesus referred by name. On occasion Jesus spoke of David and Moses and Abraham. And one day as he looked at the lilies of the fields, he compared them to "Solomon in all his glory." From what archeologists have uncovered, this is evidently a very accurate image, for in terms of buildings built and fortifications erected and commerce expanded, the reign of the third king of Israel was indeed "a time of glory." In fact, the forty years of his reign marked the pinnacle of the nation's political career; the events in Israel's history that led up to Solomon were all on an ascending curve, and much that came afterward represented decline.

The years Solomon ruled were a true turning point for the nation. With him the heroic period of Israel's life came to an end, and the era of a real centralized monar-

chy began. Gone were the simple days when there had
been no ruler except Yahweh and the heroes he occasionally saw fit to raise up. Gone were the days of pilgrimage
in the wilderness behind the mobile "tent of meeting."
Now there was a temple in Jerusalem—rooted and un-
movable—and twelve administrative districts for the
purpose of taxation and conscription took the place of the
tribal territories. The life of Israel underwent a radical
modification during the days of "Solomon and all his
glory," and the debate goes on to this day as to whether
the net effect was positive or negative. Yet there is no de-
bating the fact that Solomon was a significant figure. He
is one of our most illustrious spiritual forebears, and
there is much of a very practical nature that we can learn
from looking more closely at his life.

We have seen in earlier chapters that the men and
women depicted in the Bible were mixed creatures like
ourselves—full of both strengths and weaknesses. The
Bible does not try to cover this up. Its account of every
major figure involves a good news/bad news polarity,
and King Solomon's story is no exception. There is much
about this man to be genuinely admired, and at the same
time there was a terrifying dimension to his existence, for
toward the end his life took a direction that should be
feared at all costs.

What is most commendable about Solomon was the
way he began his reign. It is important to realize that Solomon came to the throne differently from all the other
leaders of Israel. He was no charismatic hero who had
proved himself by extraordinary achievement. He was no
warrior like Gideon or Samson or David; in fact, he never
fought a day in his life and had been raised with "a silver
spoon in his mouth." He became king solely because his
dying father singled him out to be his successor. The el-
ders of Israel were not in on this process and had nothing
to do with Solomon's election. Therefore, this young man

faced a radically different situation at the beginning of his reign than had David, who had already been an established and recognized leader and had even been sought out by the people. Solomon was a twenty-year-old unknown suddenly thrust on Israel from above, and of all the things he could have done to prepare for the difficult problems he faced, what Solomon chose to do was the best.

In the story recorded in 1 Kings 3:3–14, God appeared to the young king in a dream and offered to give him anything he desired. Such an offer is an age-old motif in literature, and is a telling device for demonstrating an individual's true nature. If all possibilities are open and there are no limits, then what one chooses in such a moment is an accurate reflection of what he or she really is and of what he or she truly values in life. In such a moment of testing, Solomon came through with flying colors, for he knew himself and his situation well enough to realize what he needed most. He asked for wisdom, for an understanding mind, for the ability to discern between good and evil so that he might be able to govern effectively and do the job that had been laid upon him by destiny. When you stop and think about it, of all the things a human being needs, what Solomon asked for is most basic. Wisdom—the ability to see things realistically and then "put them all together"—lies at the foundation of every other achievement. It is the practical skill of knowing how to make life in the deepest sense of that term "work."

Now the amazing thing is that Solomon recognized the value of wisdom so early in his life. Ask most twenty-year-olds what they would like most, and I am guessing they would opt for some of the more surface realities of life, such as fame or wealth or power. But Solomon realized that none of these things could be sustained or utilized effectively without the prior quality of wisdom, which is the key that unlocks all the rest. For example, of what lasting joy is it to have a lot of money or power if one does not know what to do with it, if the wisdom to use it well is lacking?

The primacy of wisdom is something most people eventually come to realize, but usually only after many failures. The Prodigal Son, for example, when he started out, did not ask for wisdom, but only for power and money and freedom. He was obsessed for a while with being able to do as he pleased, and then he turned out *not* to be pleased with what he had done! He finally realized that what he needed most was not more power or money or freedom, but wisdom to know how to handle all these things. Then he came back home looking for what Solomon had recognized from the very beginning as most important. This is what I admire so about the young king. He was mature for his age in recognizing what the primal human need really is.

The biblical writer indicates that God was delighted with Solomon's request and moved to answer it immediately. This says to me that we do not have to struggle against God to meet this primal need. As the book of James puts it, "If any of you lacks wisdom, let him ask God, who gives to all men generously and without reproaching, and it will be given him" (1:5, RSV). The ability "to put it all together" is not something God jealously keeps to himself. Something of the wisdom that was able to create this world in such a way that it was very good is available to anyone who, like Solomon, is willing to admit he or she needs it and who will collaborate with God in receiving it. Solomon, then, is rightly famous for his wisdom, and it is the thing about him I admire most and want to emulate in my own life.

Yet, as I said earlier, there are shadows as well as light about this man's experience, and we begin to see this as we trace out the whole course of his life. In an earlier chapter we noted that Israel's first king, Saul, began brilliantly, only to wind up in failure, and the same thing happened to Solomon. The reign that was inaugurated in the full favor of God ended forty years later with the kingdom falling apart and Solomon's own soul deeply estranged from his Maker. What happened to cause such promise to dissipate into tragedy? One explanation seems to loom larger than all others—that somewhere in the middle of his life Solomon *stopped growing.* The process of development he had begun so brilliantly he did not continue, and what always happens under such circumstances occurred—a process of disintegration set in. Our options in life are only two: either we keep on growing or we start decaying. At some point after he had already achieved considerable success, Solomon stopped the one and began the other.

Could it be that he failed to realize that the challenges of life go on into the afternoon and evening of our existence and are not just confined to the morning? The psychologist Erik Erikson has gone to great lengths to show that this human life of ours is one unending developmental cycle, and that at each stage along the way there are challenges to be met and growth to be facilitated. There is no resting place, no plateau where we can sit down and stop growing. The challenges of life go on, right up to our last breath. And unless we realize this fact, we, like Solomon, can very well lose toward the end of life what we have spent all our days building.

Part of the problem is that the challenges in the morning of life are better known and more dramatic and thus tend to monopolize our attention. The need to discover our identity, to get an education, to select a mate, to choose a vocation, to get off to a good start in our career are highly visible challenges, and it is obvious that everything afterwards depends on them. But what has not been emphasized enough is that the afternoon and evening of life present challenges, too—challenges that are different, to be sure, but just as crucial.

For instance, what happens after we have negotiated the first tests well and achieved a measure of success? Then comes what is now becoming known as "the mid-adult crisis." Here is where discontent and boredom can overwhelm us. Either we have achieved the goals we set out to achieve, and there seem to be no more worlds to conquer, or we realize that we are never going to reach those heights of attainment, and a sense of despair sets in. This is when so many marriages break up, so many careers get disrupted, so many gains that have been painstakingly achieved get tossed aside in one irrational outburst. The mid-adult crisis can be every bit as traumatic as the passage out of adolescence. And perhaps even more challenging to negotiate is the crisis of growing old—learning to simplify life and how to make the final act of trust, which is death.

Any sports fan knows that a game can be lost in the last quarter as well as the first. This is true in life as well, and this appears to be what happened to Solomon. I am still haunted by that sentence in the eleventh chapter of 1 Kings: "When Solomon was old [he] turned away his heart after other gods" (v. 4). The first ten chapters of this book chronicle Solomon's successes—how humble and teachable he was at the beginning, how open he was to God's guidance, how wise and understanding he was as a ruler. And then, after all this, he lapsed into failure when he may have thought all the crucial moments of his life were over. All this occurred when he was old!

This is a sobering thought to me, and underlines again the fact that all of life matters. If the experience of Solomon teaches us anything, it is that the challenge to keep on growing never ends. It is not he who just begins well who succeeds; it is he "who endureth to the end [who] shall be saved" (Matt. 10:22, KJV). This means there is no resting place, no point in life when we can let up spiritually and sit back and say, "I have it made. I don't have to struggle any more. I no longer have to worry about being faithful to God." There is no mistake more fatal than to stop growing. The years after forty, after sixty—even after eighty—are still years of significance. But somewhere toward the end of his life—"when he was old"— Solomon stopped growing, and the moment that happened disintegration set in. Never forget—if this could happen to Solomon, it could happen to you and me. None of us are immune to the danger of not continuing to grow.

Solomon's experience, then, is foreboding because of *when* his downfall occurred, but equally disturbing is what got him off the track. It would appear that what Percy Bysshe Shelley called "the world's slow stain" finally engulfed Solomon. His wives with their foreign religions had some influence over him, but it seems that the lure of materialism was an even stronger factor. Toward the end Solomon became obsessed with luxury and comfort and ostentation. This may have all begun innocently in his desire to build a Temple to the Lord—something his father David had longed to do but had been unable to fulfill. Solomon very responsibly picked up the momentum of his heritage and carried it forward, but in the very process of designing and structuring this building a love of things seems to have taken deep root in his heart. He no longer saw objects in the functional sense of how they could serve God and humankind; he began to revere them as ends in themselves and to value them for what they could mean in terms of his comfort and prestige and grandeur.

A tiny clue that something was happening in the soul of Solomon can be found in the fact that he spent seven years building the Temple and then thirteen years constructing his own palace, which was extravagant beyond all precedent. From then on Solomon's materialism escalated. He became more and more engrossed in material things—erecting buildings and fortifications everywhere and subverting everything to this end. As the years went by, he gradually shifted from being a wise ruler to being a compulsive builder. In the process, something deep down inside Solomon began to die, and the personal dimensions of his being hardened into insensitivity.

This decline can be documented by comparing two events from different eras of Solomon's life. As a young king his great concern was for a discerning heart to govern his people wisely. It was obvious that what happened to his subjects was his first concern, and he demonstrated great sensitivity towards them. For example, one day two harlots were brought to him to settle a dispute. These two lived together and both had had babies at about the same time. One night one of them had rolled over on her infant and smothered him, and when she had realized it she had exchanged infants with the other woman. On awakening, the second woman had realized that the dead baby was not hers, and the two of them had gotten into a terrible conflict over the identity of the remaining child. When Solomon heard this case, he ordered his sword brought out and proposed to cut in two the living infant and give a half to each one of the contestants. The suggestion caught both women by surprise, and one of them quickly cried, "Oh no, don't do that; give her the baby rather than kill him!" The other woman agreed to the proposal. Immediately Solomon pronounced that the woman who had protested was the true mother and awarded her the child, for the test of love had shrewdly brought the truth to light.

Solomon showed in this instance that he was well acquainted with the workings of the human heart—how a mother would feel toward the prospect of her child being murdered. Compare his sensitivity at this point to a time years later when, in order to get his extensive projects built, he had to resort to slave labor. He began by shackling conquered foreigners into servitude, but by the time it was over, Solomon was enslaving his own people as well. At the height of his building mania, the Bible says he had over one hundred fifty-three thousand people under yoke.

What had happened to the human sensitivity that at one time had been able to feel with a harlot mother but was now utterly callous to the fact that more than one hundred thousand people were being "cut in two" by slavery? The answer, I am afraid, is that Solomon had been made over in the image of the "god" he had come to worship.

We must never forget the awesome creative power that resides in ultimate devotion. We are always being made in the image of our "god"; inevitably we become like that which we worship. Therefore, what we prize most is for that very reason the greatest creative force in our lives. Back when I was in the seminary, they used to tell about a former professor who had been wounded in World War I and who had carried his right shoulder at a much lower angle than the left. He had been an exceedingly popular professor, and it was said that at any graduation time a good three-fourths of the graduates would come across the stage to receive their diplomas with an identical but affected slope of the shoulder.

Such is the creative power of devotion—which explains why as long as Solomon was in close touch with Yahweh he stayed sensitive to people. To the Father-Creator, it is human beings who matter most; to him the highest of all values are personal values. However, when the "slow stain" of materialism gradually gained ascendancy in Solomon's heart, he began to assume the features of that functional deity; that is, he became hard and unfeeling just as material things are hard and unfeeling. The basic direction of divine creation was reversed, and Solomon became dehumanized. It is God's pattern to take the material and to personalize it until at last all inorganic things are caught up in the personal dimension. It is the work of the demonic, however, to undo this process, to take the personal and gradually materialize it until human beings become like things. When Solomon turned his heart away from the true God and began to place too much value on affluence and luxury and the building of buildings, his concern for people evaporated and he became an unfeeling tyrant.

Many of us in our day are vulnerable to this same temptation. We are surrounded by affluence to such a degree that the easiest thing in the world to do is to start valuing things more than human beings, and thus to lose our true humanity. Each of us needs to ask the simple question: When it comes right down to it, which am I willing to sacrifice—things for people or people for things? When I have to make a choice, which is the end and which the means? The Bible is utterly clear in saying that we are made in the image of a personal, caring God, and that the grand sign of our maturing in his image is our growing sensitivity to people, our learning to make the material the servant of the personal and not the other way around.

I am haunted again and again by Jesus' parable of the Last Judgment (Matt. 25), in which he indicates that the ultimate difference between those who will be saved and those who will not be saved will be this one issue of what is most important. Who will be those whom the Son of Man will place on his right—those who will be invited to inherit the kingdom of joy prepared for them from the foundations of the earth? They will be the ones who have been willing to sacrifice things for the good of people. "I was hungry and you gave me to eat; I was thirsty and you gave me to drink; I was naked and you clothed me.

Inasmuch as you invested your things in the least of these my brethren, you were doing something for me, yea, you were acting the way I would have acted." But those on the left will be those who have done just the opposite—those who have sacrificed people in the interest of things. "When did we see you hungry, thirsty, naked?" they will ask. They will be the people who, like Solomon, grew insensitive to the personal, and therefore there will be no place for them in a realm where what matters most is people. They will miss it because, like Solomon, they let their hearts be turned away to other gods. Instead of becoming like him in whose image they were originally made, they became something he never intended—hard, cold, unfeeling objects.

Therefore, let every person take heed of our kinsman, Solomon. He started out so brilliantly and then—when he was old, in the last quarter of his life—he lost it all. If this could happen to Solomon, what right do any of us have to think it could not happen to us? It could, my friend, it could!

18

OUR SHADOW SELVES

Romans 7:15–25

SOME TIME AGO I was given a gift that has proved quite useful to me in trying to understand my day-to-day life. This gift was the concept of "our many selves." Put quite simply, that phrase means that a human being is not just one thing, but a combination of many things. There are numerous facets to my being; I am a veritable parliament of personhood. And this is why my daily experiences are never simple or the making of decisions easy. There are many voices inside me clamoring to be heard and many forces struggling against each other within my internal establishment. Therefore, there will never be perfect unanimity or a lack of conflict within me, for I am not just one self; I am many selves at once.

Now, to be honest, this particular way of talking about personality came as something new to me, but then again, it was not totally alien. The image of "many selves" immediately linked up with an experience I had had many times since my earliest childhood—that of

173

having many different inclinations all at once. It also linked up well with what the Bible says about human nature. Again and again this document makes reference to the many "selves" that are at work within the human personality.

For example, there is Elijah in the Old Testament saying to the Israelites on Mount Carmel, "How long will you go limping with two different opinions? If the Lord is God, follow him; but if Baal, then follow him" (1 Kings 18:21). The Israelites' indecision is a clear illustration of that dividedness one feels within one's being when one is caught in the crossfire of alternative powers and pulled first this way and then that.

We find the same reality in an even more dramatic form when Jesus asks the Gadarene demoniac his name and the man replies, "My name is legion, for there are many of us" (Mark 5:9, PHILLIPS). This man is an extreme example of the multiplicity of selves existing in one person. In his case, the many facets had gotten completely out of hand and open civil war had erupted, which meant this man was utterly fragmented and reduced to living among the tombs like a raving maniac.

Paul refers to the same condition in the seventh chapter of Romans, in which he lays bare his soul and admits that at times he is a mystery even to himself. He says,

The good that I would I do not: but the evil which I would not, that I do. Now if I do that I would not, it is no more I that do it, but sin that dwelleth in me. I find then a law, that, when I would do good, evil is present with me. For I delight in the law of God after the inward man: But I see another law in my members, warring against the law of my mind, and bringing me into captivity to the law of sin which is in my members. O wretched man that I am! who shall deliver me from the body of this death? (Rom. 7:19–24, KJV).

I can still remember reading these words in late adolescence—how they seemed to leap out at me. I felt I was looking into a giant mirror; what Paul was describing was precisely my predicament—experiencing myself as more than one, setting out to do one thing and winding up doing the opposite.

This, then, is why I said the concept of "our many selves" made sense to me the first time I ever read it. It gave shape and form to something I had been experiencing for many years but did not really understand, and I believe it can serve the same purpose in your life. This gift which I have found useful I now want to pass on to you, for I believe that to the degree that you want to know yourself and be on a pilgrimage with Jesus Christ toward personal maturity, this way of understanding how the human personality works cannot help but be beneficial.

I have found that this concept does two things for me. First, it helps me acknowledge the truth about my own situation—that I am a multiplicity of selves, not just one thing but many things. And second, it opens a way for me to start getting acquainted with all those "shadow selves" that I vaguely sense exist within me but that are not really known or understood or controlled by me.

Now, as long as I think of myself as only one, this kind of healthy self-discovery is not possible. In fact, what happens is that I will become so baffled by the multiplicity within me or so ashamed at having all these conflicting feelings that I will resort to unhealthy ways of coping with myself and will wind up making matters worse instead of better.

For example, one time-honored way of dealing with our "shadow selves" is to deny them—to simply turn our backs on certain things within us that we find too painful or shameful to admit, refusing to acknowledge that they even exist. This is precisely how Simon Peter tried to cope the night of our Lord's betrayal. There on the Mount of Olives Jesus shared what he saw to be approaching—that he would be handed over to his enemies and that all the disciples would desert him. I do not see this as an iron-clad prediction of what had to happen; I believe rather that it was Jesus' evaluation of what would probably happen, given the condition of the disciples right then. Thus, in a way, it was a challenge. Jesus was telling these men something about themselves they obviously did not know, hoping, I imagine, that they would realize it and join him in trying to prepare for the ordeal by praying to God the Father.

However, Peter was too frightened by such a prospect even to hear the challenge. The thought of his having in him the capacity to desert his best friend in an hour of crisis was too awful even to acknowledge, so he denied this shadow self vehemently. "Oh no, Jesus," he cried. "These others may desert you, but not me. I'm prepared to stick with you all the way, even if it means death." Jesus must have thought to himself, "Peter, how little you really know about all that is within you." He told Peter, "Before the cock crows three times in the morning, you will have denied me," which, of course, is exactly what happened.

You see, when Peter refused to acknowledge the existence of that shadow self that had the capacity to betray a friend, he was in effect turning himself over to its power and laying himself at its mercy. This is what we always do when we deny or repress those aspects of ourselves we find too objectionable to admit. Instead of getting rid of these realities, we simply turn them loose to roam the darkness of our unconscious as they will, which means they can create ten times as much havoc as would be possible if they were acknowledged openly. Anyone who has ever had a real enemy knows the pain of having to face up to that fact, but also the wisdom of keeping such a one under surveillance rather than having him lurk about in the darkness. Had Simon Peter been willing to face up to the fact that he was many selves, and that part of him was cowardly and capable of "cutting out when the crunch was on," he might have then mobilized the parts of him that really did want to be faithful. The technique of denial prevented this.

I have often wondered if Peter was anywhere around when Jesus prayed from the cross, "Father forgive them, for they know not what they do." This was exactly Simon Peter's problem. What he did not know did hurt him! He was at the mercy of his shadow self, doing what he really had not intended to do, precisely because he refused to acknowledge and to deal with all that was within him. We are never in greater danger than in those moments when we think we are incapable of certain types of behavior. Blocking out the parts of us we fear serves only to make us more vulnerable than ever to the darkness we so painfully dread. If you think the way of denial is the way to deal with your shadow selves, have a look at Simon Peter and at what came of his brash denial. I think you will agree that there is no health or hope down this road.

Neither is there hope along another time-honored path—that of projecting our shadow selves on other people and trying to destroy our darkness by attacking them. This is what I see happening in the episode in John's Gospel in which the woman caught in the act of adultery was dragged before Jesus. The teachers of the Law and the Pharisees said accusingly, "Moses says such a one ought to be stoned. What do you say?" The way our Lord responded to this situation leads me to feel that it was not just what the woman had done, but what this made these men feel about themselves, that really upset them. Therefore, Jesus deftly shifted the focus to the real problem and said, "All right, whoever of you is without sin in this area, let him be the executor of Moses' Law. Let him cast the first stone."

In turning the issue back from the accused to the accusers, Jesus was putting his finger on what was actually happening. These men were attempting to get at the darkness in their own lives by projecting it on another and trying to destroy her. This is the age-old practice of "protesting too much," and recognizing it ought to trigger searching self-examination on the part of each of us into those areas where we tend to be quick to condemn and often feel called on to mount a crusade. Why are we indignant about this or that particular fault in another? Is it because we sense this same problem in ourselves and yet cannot face it? Instead of doing battle inside, where the real problem is, do we go to war against another human being? This tactic is an attempt to substitute darkness without for darkness within, and it never really solves anything, although it is always being tried by "crusader types" who never realize that what they are actually fighting is something within their own selves. The comic-strip character Pogo summed up this approach long ago when he said, "We have met the enemy and he is us." This is often the truth behind our condemnations. And if we fail to recognize this truth, the prayer of Jesus is again applicable: "Father forgive them, for they know not what they do."

I hope it is clear by now that neither denial nor projecting are really healthy ways of coping with our shadow selves—which is why I find the concept of "many selves" so helpful. I repeat, here is a way of understanding our experience and doing something about it! Here is an invitation to acknowledge that we are many, and then to set about the task of getting acquainted with and doing something about those parts of us we would like to deny. You see, these are precisely the parts of us that need to be redeemed, and redemption according to Christ is always a process of light and love.

This is precisely the kind of mission Jesus undertook when he came to earth to save us from our sin. By his own admission, he did not come to destroy anything, but rather to redeem and transform what had become twisted and distorted. The premise behind his approach is the doctrine of creation, which claims that nothing is really bad in itself. Everything bad is something good that has been misshapen or perverted. And this applies to our shadow selves, those aspects of our being which we do not know and which we greatly fear. This is precisely the part of us which Christ came to heal, so that we could at last come into possession of our whole selves and be able to fulfill the first and greatest commandment, to love the Lord our God—how?—with all of our heart and mind and soul and strength. In a word, with all our many selves!

Christ has two very specific words as to how this redemption is to take place. The first is, "Resist not evil" (Matt. 5:39, KJV). That is, do not deny or project those facets of our selves that seem evil, but acknowledge them for what they are and listen to what they have to say. If we do this—that is, really feel our feelings—they may be able to tell us a great deal about our true condition and need. For example, there may be a part of us that is ruthlessly greedy for material things. No matter how much we have, something inside wants more. It is by no means pleasant or satisfying to admit that this sort of reality exists within us. Yet if we do admit it, if we don't deny or project this part of us, we may discover from this shadow self that we are suffering from acute inner poverty, that because we get so little satisfaction out of our personal beings we are trying to compensate by acquiring things. Or again, there may be a jealous self in us, particularly toward creative and gifted people. And when we "resist not" this dark messenger, when we let him have his say, we come to realize he speaks for the creative gifts buried deep in us that we have never uncovered and begun to use. Painful as it is, acknowledging and listening to these shadow selves can show us things about ourselves we could never know any other way.

The other word of Jesus regarding our shadow selves is a more familiar one: "Love your enemies, bless them that curse you, do good to them that . . . despitefully use you" (Matt. 5:44, KJV). What I am suggesting is that Christ would have us not destroy those twisted selves, but embrace them—kiss them, if you please—and thus transform them and redirect their energies positively. Perhaps the reason they got lost in the first place was a lack of love. After all, is not the fear of rejection the reason we hide parts of ourselves? Deep in all of us is the assumption that, if we were fully known, we would be condemned and cut off forever.

Yet this is precisely the fear Jesus Christ came to cast out. Remember, he is the One about whom it was written, "He knew what was in man" (John 2:25, KJV). No one had to tell Jesus anything about human nature; he knew it more profoundly than any other. And yet this is the same One who loved people so completely. Jesus Christ is the One who puts it all together. He is God's great declaration that we are accepted even when we are fully known. If the love of Christ had been combined with ignorance or naïveté about human nature, things would be different. But the Good News is that he who knows us best is the same One who loves us the most! Thus we can venture forth to love our enemies—those ugly, twisted shapes that have for so long huddled in our darkness. We can love them with a new kind of courage and tenderness, because Christ has first loved them even while they were yet sinners, and so we can follow him into ourselves.

A great symbol of the hope the love of Christ can bring to our shadow selves is what happened to Francis of Assisi early in his ministry. He had always had a terrible a-version to the disease of leprosy and could hardly bring himself even to look on a person who was so afflicted. One day as he was riding along, he suddenly confronted a leper who cried out for help. Francis's first reaction was one of utter repulsion, but then with an act of courage greater even than a soldier's daring in battle, he dismounted and embraced the pitiful creature. As he did this, he got his first glimpse of the leper's face and, according to the story, what he saw was the countenance of Christ himself!

This story symbolizes, I think, the fact that when we dare to embrace those parts of ourselves that are most distasteful, what we discover is that here is something Christ loves and has already identified with and wants to redeem. It is through Christ, then, that we get the challenge and the courage to face our shadow selves and embrace them. Elizabeth O'Conner says the Great Commission can be understood internally as well as externally. Christ calls us to go into all the parts of our inner world, making disciples of all our selves, and baptizing them in the name of the Father and the Son and the Holy Ghost. This means lifting the sunken continents of our being out of the murky waters of unconsciousness into the light, so that finally we can "bless the Lord with all that is within us."

This is at least part of the redemptive mission which Christ came to earth to accomplish, and the concept of "our many selves" has helped him carry out this mission in me. By acknowledging I am many, not just one, and that I must not resist my many selves, but love them, I find a reason for the greatest adventure of all—discovering all that God has made me to be and seeking to collaborate with him in the finishing of the task of my creation.

19

WHAT DO YOU
DO WITH YOUR SINS?

Isaiah 1:18; Psalm 103:10–11;
1 John 1:9

JUST BEFORE THE OUTBREAK OF WORLD WAR I, a noted British psychologist said, "Twentieth-century human beings are no longer troubled about their sins. They regard this category as a hangover from the primitive past. They have outgrown such a concept." It was amazing how quickly that statement was picked up and quoted in journal after jounal. It seemed to epitomize how at least the intellectual community of that day understood the human situation. However, as the decades since then have unfolded it has become apparent that if twentieth-century human beings are not troubled about their sins, they certainly are troubled about something! Has there ever been an age of greater anxiety or turbulence or unrest than these past eight decades?

To be sure, words like *sin* and *guilt* and *forgiveness* are no longer widely used in many circles, but does that mean the realities to which they referred have disappeared? I think not! In fact, if you listen today to

183

twentieth-century human beings describe their situation, you'll notice that words like *phobia* and *complexes* and *neuroses* punctuate the conversation; in my opinion, they are referring to the same realities once described by the older names. What has changed is not our human situation, but simply our terminology.

People today, like people in every era, are an imperfect lot. We fail and falter and stumble. We break with values and ideals and people that are very dear to us, and whenever we do this a situation is created that has to be dealt with in some way. Just as bleeding automatically follows a laceration of the skin, so guilt and anxiety or shame or an inferiority complex or self-loathing or whatever you want to call it follows a violation of the structure of value in which life is set. We are all by nature value-cherishing creatures. Certain principles and ideals are important to us, and it follows that we cannot do violence to these and walk away untouched. In such moments, we may not like words such as *sin* or *guilt*, but what we cannot deny is that something is going on within us and that some response has to be made to this turbulence.

Few people saw as deeply into life in the twentieth century as the poet T. S. Eliot. In his lengthy work entitled *The Cocktail Party*, he pictures a woman named Celia talking to her psychiatrist, Reilly, about a certain thing she has done that is really bothering her conscience. Reilly asks her, "What was the point of view of your family about the word, *sin?*" She replies that she had been taught to disbelieve in it, to think of misbehavior as simply "bad form," and to regard anyone who was overly concerned with guilt as a bit "kinky." But then she admits that she had been unable to dispose of her sense of personal failure so easily. She says, "I continue to be bothered by a feeling of uncleanness, a feeling of emptiness, of failure toward someone or something outside myself. And I feel I must . . . atone, is that the word? Tell me, can you treat a patient for such a state of mind?"

Here is poignant evidence that twentieth-century human beings are indeed troubled about their sins, even though they may not use that word for it any more. And this is the issue to which I want to speak now. What do we do with that sense of failure that comes over us when we break faith with those realities that are most important in our lives, when we do the things we ourselves believe we should not do, or leave undone the things we ourselves believe we should have done? There is no question of more practical importance to any of us than how we go about dealing with that special sense of failure called "guilt."

I have seen people attempt to handle this problem in a variety of ways. The most common, I suppose, is the strategy of evading and avoiding guilt, of finding a sense of failure so painful that one represses it and hopes in childlike fantasy that it will go away. Unfortunately, reality does not work that way, for when something as significant as guilt is banished from consciousness, it simply moves into the unconscious and begins to roam unchecked in the foundations of one's being, only to resurface later in more hideous forms.

The celebrated case that first got Sigmund Freud started in psychoanalysis was that of a young woman in her late teens who was paralyzed from the waist down. No physical cause could be found for this condition. Then, by chance, because of a remark she made about a dream, he began to explore her subconscious through hypnosis. He found that several years before this woman had "buried" an awesome experience of guilt. As a young girl, she had fallen in love with the husband of her older sister, and in adolescent fantasy had wished one day that her sister would die so she could marry her handsome brother-in-law. Not long after that, the sister had died suddenly. The young woman had been so overwhelmed with guilt for having wished this and so fearful that her desire had caused it that she had been deeply troubled.

She had not been able to face what she felt was a shameful sin, and so she had repressed it, and not long afterwards had developed paralysis. Freud realized that these physical symptoms were in fact a form of self-punishment and also a protection against going any further down a forbidden path. All of this was going on "out of sight," mind you, because the woman had evaded her guilt, only to have it reappear in an even worse, more grotesque form.

The warning of the Bible rings clearly here: "Be sure your sin will find you out" (Num. 32:23). You cannot ignore sin just because it is distasteful. Disposing of guilt by evasion is a way of dealing with it—but an utterly disastrous one; you might as well gather up the termites you find in the living room and deal with them by turning them loose in your basement! Guilt will not be denied or dismissed so easily.

I have seen other people attempt to get rid of guilt by disclaiming responsibility for it, like Adam did when he passed the blame to Eve and then Eve did by pointing a finger at the snake. This is a way of saying, "It was not my fault. Someone else did this to me and made me do it." Such excuses, which imply that human beings are mere leaves in the wind, devoid of any power of their own, are always wide of the mark. This is not the way we talk when we have done something good! On those occasions we want credit and praise, as rightly we should, for while it is true that none of us are totally free, yet at the same time the freedom we do have is genuine. After all, Adam and Eve were influenced, but not coerced, to partake of that tree. What was done to them they allowed to be done; they had a voice in what was decided. We are living in a time when blame is very much in fashion, but it is an inferior way of resolving the tension of guilt. It is a solution that solves too much, for it is achieved only at the expense of significant personhood.

The same inadequacy holds true for the strategy of projection—when we see a reflection of our own problem in
another and attempt to cleanse ourselves of our guilt by
condemning or destroying that person. As I noted in the
previous chapter, this is what I believe the scribes and
Pharisees were doing the day they brought the adulter-
ous woman to Jesus and wanted to stone her. Jesus
would not let them get away with such projection. "The
problem here," he said, "is not just her but also you.
What she did must have made you uncomfortable about
certain tendencies within yourselves. Go work on your
own problems. Reformation begins at home."

Another strategy for dealing with guilt is trying to relativize it by saying that lots of people do this same thing,
so why get so upset? This is a very common practice, but
it cannot succeed, because it comes at the problem of
guilt from a totally wrong perspective. After all, the profound realities of right and wrong have never been determined by a popular vote. Where guilt is concerned, it is
really irrelevant to say, "Lots of others do the same thing,
so forget it."

I once had to minister to a man who had just run over
and killed his three-year-old son. This man had been
watching a baseball game on television and had drunk
too many beers, and when he and his wife got into an ar-
gument he stormed out and started the car. He did not
see his little son running after him until it was too late. I
shall never forget the horror on his face as he told me
about looking over the hood and seeing the body of his
child in the driveway. Of what comfort would it have
been for me to say, "You know, I read the other day of
two other fathers who did the same thing. You're not the
only one. Forget it." In such a moment, what other
people do or do not do is irrelevant. We can always find
somebody better or worse than ourselves, but that is not
the point. This is why the Bible calls on us to love the

Lord with all our hearts and souls and minds and strength (Mark 12:30). We are to get our bearings from him, not from other people. Relativizing away our guilt will never really work.

By all odds the most noble strategy for dealing with guilt is the way of self-punishment. Do you remember how T. S. Eliot's Celia said, "I feel I must atone for this"? This is a very deep impulse of the human spirit—to conclude that because a wrong has been done, some price needs to be paid or some equivalent action taken. At least in this approach there is a recognition of the seriousness of the situation and of the individual's responsibility. However, the problem with self-punishment is that one never knows how much is enough; we can spend all our lives scourging ourselves and still feel no sense of absolution. Soren Kierkegaard's father, as a shepherd lad out on the freezing Danish slopes, once cursed God, and the memory of that act of blasphemy haunted the man for the rest of his life. He never stopped punishing himself for this misdeed. He gave lavish sums of money to the church, even lacerated his own body, but he was never able to believe that the debt had at last been paid. Any attempt to design or effect our own atonement is bound to end in uncertainty and failure. For example, what could that father I mentioned a moment ago ever have done to "make up" for the killing of his child? Like the spots on Lady Macbeth's hand, guilt will not be removed by anything we are able to do.

Here, then, are just a few of the ways I have seen people struggle with that special sense of failure called guilt. Yet not one of these, actually, is "a solution that really solves," for the simple reason that each one is an attempt to resolve the sin problem with human resources alone. As I have already intimated, this cannot be done. In and of ourselves, we do not have the power to take our sins, though they be "as scarlet," and wash them "white as snow" (see Isa. 1:18). In order for that to happen, we must call in Another. As Jesus said, "Those who are whole have no need of a physician. But those who are sick and guilty—ah, that is another matter" (see Mark 2:17). For them, the only hope for disposing of guilt and getting on with life lies in a Power beyond ourselves and in what he can do for them and with them.

I am talking, of course, about God, and yet what reluctance there is to involve him in this matter, for we know instinctively that, when God becomes a part of our situation, our guilt takes on a new dimension and greater complexity. For then it becomes apparent that we have not just sinned against ourselves or other people or certain ideals; we have also sinned against God, by using the bodies he has given us to violate the world he has created and to hurt the creatures he loves! Initially, getting God involved with our guilt seems only to add to the problem.

I remember quite well the night one of my high school contemporaries asked for the family car and was refused, but slipped out in it anyway and was involved in a terrible accident. I happened to drive up just after it had happened. There were three cars badly damaged and several people hurt, and my friend standing in a daze beside it all. He told me how frightened he was to call his folks and tell them what had happened. You see, in addition to all the damage and injury he had caused, there was also the problem of a breach of trust with his parents. This is exactly what happens initially when we think of calling God into our situation of guilt. Added to everything else we have done is the fact that we have broken faith with him as well. This realization causes many people to draw back and refuse to take their sins to God. But nothing could be more tragic, for in truth it is what seems at first to add to the problem that turns out to be a real solution.

Going back to my friend at the scene of the accident—I urged him "to bite the bullet" and get in touch with his father. "Hard as it is," I said, "it is the only way." So we went to the nearest house. I dialed the number and handed him the phone and saw him do an awesome thing—he "confessed" to his father what he had done and what had happened, and he cried for help. What followed was a beautiful example of merciful humanity. Within minutes that father was at the scene. The very first thing he did was embrace that trembling boy and assure him that his love was not a conditional thing, but a bond of grace. Then he made all his resources available to deal with the problems that always have to be faced in the wake of a sin or a failure. There was the challenge of restitution, of what could be done to set right the wrong that had been done—in this case, the injured people and the damaged property. And deeper still was the challenge of reclamation of what could be done about the wrong in the boy that had made him disobey and get involved in the accident. How could he be changed so this kind of tragedy would not recur? For all the father's love and acceptance and willingness to help, it was obvious that the boy had an agenda of restitution and reclamation to work through if this misfortune were to be moved through creatively and redemptively.

I have often thought of that experience as a parable of the Christian gospel. It is very much like Jesus' story of the Prodigal Son, for which facing up to reality and calling in the help of the Father proved to be the turning point. The only real solution I know for that special sense of failure called guilt begins with acknowledging the sin we have committed—not trying to evade it or blame it on someone else or project it or relativize it or atone for it by ourselves. First we "own" our sin, and then we make that painful telephone call to the Father and "ask him into our mess." This is never as bad as we might fear, for just as the Prodigal's old father came running to meet him as soon as he made his first move to return, so the Father of all Mercies will respond to us if we move toward him. For, you see, his is an unconditional love; it does not depend on how well or how poorly we do. Our relationship to God was not created by what we did, but by what he did, and no amount of sin can break that bond.

Neither can sin eliminate God's hope for our future. The real meaning of mercy is that it can look on failure and still see a future, the way the Prodigal's father did when he called for the ring and the robe and the shoes. This is the great thing the Father of Mercies does for us—he gives us hope. Our sins have a way of creating self-loathing and self-despair. The Prodigal, for instance, had just about given up on what he could ever become. Given his track record, a hired servant's future was about all he thought he could expect. Yet his father's forgiveness changed all that; it set a new future before him on the same terms as the past—that is, as a free gift—and invited him to get on with the business of restitution and reclamation and personal growth. The same thing happens to us when we dare to go to our Father with our guilt.

It is important to realize that the efforts we make to repair the damage we have done and to undergo growth within ourselves are not something we do in order to earn forgiveness, but something we undertake *because we have been forgiven*. They are the consequences, not the conditions, of redemption; there is all the difference in the world between these fruits of forgiveness and our futile attempts at self-atonement. For example, my friend who ran over his child finally did call in God and accept his forgiveness and allow him to wash him "whiter than snow." But do you know what he has been doing ever since? He has been the mover in one of the most successful Boy Scout movements in all of the South, doing for other boys what he could never do for his own son. And he is not doing it, mind you, in order to earn God's mercy, but because that mercy was given.

This is an authentic sign to me that my friend's guilt has really been dealt with. Where there is no reaching out to God, no accepting of decisive mercy, no impulse toward restitution, or no desire for inward change, then even the hands of a God of mercy are tied. But when the call does go out—"Father, I have sinned against heaven and before your sight"—God responds by giving hope, helping with restitution, and initiating growth within. Then the promises of Scripture are fulfilled: "Though your sins be as scarlet, they shall be as white as snow" (Isaiah 1:18, KJV) . . . "As far as the east is from the west, so far hath he removed our sins from us" (Psalm 103:12, KJV) . . . "He is faithful and just to forgive us our sins and to cleanse us from all unrighteousness" (1 John 1:9, KJV). What I am saying is that the only answer to the sin problem is the Father, and the only way to deal with our guilt is to go to him as the Prodigal turned toward home and gave himself over to mercy and to restitution and to reformation.

Myron Madden once observed that we either accept the atonement God has provided us in Jesus Christ or we attempt to enact our own atonement, and this sums up what I have tried to say in this chapter. We twentieth-century people are no different from third-century ones when we break faith with the deepest realities of our existence; the condition of guilt results just as bleeding follows an open cut. We have no choice but to make some response; to attempt not to deal with it is simply to deal with it unproductively. And we do not have the power to resolve the problem of guilt on our own—not by burying it or disclaiming it or relativizing it or projecting it or punishing ourselves. As far as I know, there is only one way—to take our guilt to the Great Physician who, when called in and allowed to do his work in us, never disappoints. Jesus has already paid for atonement. Either we accept what he has done and will do for us and find our sin problem resolved, or in many and various ways we attempt to deal with the problem ourselves, and again and again we fail.

Do you remember what it was the self-made man once said? "If I had it all to do over again, I'd call in some help!" That is the best suggestion I know of in relation to the problem of guilt. Call in help—God's help—here and now.

20

GOD FOR EACH OF US

Exodus 20:1–2; Luke 10:25–28

ONE OF THE MOST VIVID MEMORIES of my early childhood was the time my grandparents from Mississippi came to spend the winter with us in Tennessee. I must have been four or five at the time, for I was not old enough to read by myself, but I did enjoy having others read to me. That winter proved to be "a golden time" in that regard, for my grandfather was under no pressure and we would spend hour after hour before the fireplace in the living room reading all kinds of material. One of my favorites was *Hurlbut's Story of the Bible*. Like most children, I developed a special liking for certain stories and asked that they be read and reread again and again.

One such favorite was the Old Testament account of Moses and the plagues. It is not hard to understand why this material would appeal to a child, because it is full of drama and excitement. Moses went down to Egypt and, in the name of Yahweh, demanded that the Pharaoh allow the children of Israel to go free. The ruler replied that he was sorry, but he did not believe he had ever met this particular deity. Then his mood turned nasty. He told Moses to get out of there and stop tampering with his slaves. That turned out to be a bad mistake on the Pharaoh's part, for this Yahweh proceeded to introduce himself by sending plague after plague on the whole land of Egypt. These were really bizarre affairs. One time the Nile River turned to blood, then there were invasions of frogs and locusts and flies, and finally the first-born son of Pharaoh was struck dead. Every time one of these plagues would get unbearable, Pharaoh would relent and promise to release the Hebrew people. But as soon as the pressure was off, he would renege or, as the book of Exodus says, would "harden his heart" and go back on his word. This went on back and forth for months; in fact, through a series of ten different plagues, and I used to get my grandfather to read the account of this struggle over and over again.

However, when I became an adult, the same story that had delighted me as a child began to raise serious intellectual and religious problems. By this time I was not looking to the Bible for entertainment, but for insight, for clues into the nature of ultimate reality. I would find myself asking, "What was the God of the Bible doing in all of this? In the end Yahweh had to liberate the Hebrews forcefully; why did he not go ahead and do this at the beginning and forego the futile "game of the plagues"? As I studied the passage more carefully, however, I discovered something I had not known before, something that gave this account a whole new perspective. I learned that each of these plagues involved something the Egyptians regarded as divine. These people were polytheists; that is, they did not believe in just one God, but rather in many, many gods. They worshipped the Nile River, the sun, the Pharaoh and his family, and they even thought of frogs and locusts and flies as being manifestations of divinity. This discovery shed a whole different light for me on the story of the plagues, for it suggested that God was doing something more in all this than just trying to deliver his chosen people from bondage. In a real sense, he was trying to deliver the Egyptians from a form of bondage also—by educating them at the most important level of life, the religious level. He was trying to show them who really was God.

All of us probably need to sharpen our understanding of this familiar little three-letter word. The term, *god*, can be used in two very different ways. It can be used descriptively, to refer to a specific divine being who exists in his own right. Or, it can be used functionally, to refer to whatever reality a person makes most important in his or her life. Now, in the first sense there can be atheists—people who say adamantly that they do not believe in the existence of any such thing as a Divine Being. In the second sense, however, there can be no atheists, for all of us organize life around some value—some object or person or idea that we deem most important, and right here is the most crucial single issue of our lives.

Now, what if that which you are worshipping as a god—that is, looking up to and relying upon in an ultimate sense—is not in fact God—that is, does not have the power to sustain and satisfy and fulfill your life? This is at the bottom of all human tragedy—people set their ultimate hopes on that which does not have the power to save or fulfill. And when this happens, just as Jesus said, that which is "built on sand" collapses and goes to pieces and ends up in disintegration. I once saw a bumper sticker that said: "Let God be God." On first glance a phrase like that sounds like so much religious doubletalk and "gobbledegook." But on deeper reflection, I realized it stated the most important imperative of life. What could be more important, really, than letting one's god be the true God—letting the One who is God by nature function as one's god in fact?

The god-question really is life's most significant issue,

and in this light the story of the plagues really does begin to make sense. It is a dramatic parable, actually, of what is going on every day of our lives as the God who made us does battle with the gods we have made. This was "the name of the game" as Yahweh and Pharaoh squared off centuries ago. The Egyptian people had elevated all kinds of things to a godlike status—the Nile River, the sun, the Pharaoh and his family, even animals like frogs and locusts. And Yahweh took each of these in turn and demonstrated his control over them and thus superiority to them. He was trying to make one point and one point only—"Look who is and is not God." He was trying to keep these Egyptians from building their lives upon sand by making clear who really was the Rock of salvation. That remains the agenda of the God of the Bible down to this day. He is from first to last "the destroyer of the gods," not because of some infantile streak of jealousy in his nature, but because of the structure of reality and because he desires our fulfillment.

You see, the way this world is put together, there are only two forms of reality—the Creator and the creation. Only God is in the first category; he alone is the un-created One; the One who has life in himself. All the rest is creation—derived, dependent, looking to Another for its existence. It follows from this that only the Creator can fully satisfy and genuinely fulfill a creature. As St. Augustine said so long ago, "Thou has made us for thyself, O Lord, and our hearts are restless until they rest in thee."

This is the way life is put together, and this is why the practice of idolatry is always taken so seriously in Holy Scripture. It is a way of death and destruction. Why? Because it involves looking to and depending upon for salvation that which does not have the power to save. It is like a tribe in the primitive bush country of Australia that was found to be starving to death. Their main source of food was a fruit that looked good and tasted delicious but possessed no nutritional substance. Here they were depending on something for vitality that did not have vitality to give! This is the tragedy of every form of idolatry — it means relying ultimately on something that is ultimately unreliable. This is precisely what God was trying to avert in the drama of the plagues; he was attempting to unmask the pretender gods and reveal them for the unstable hopes that they were. And he has continued this "ministry of unmasking" in the experience of daily life through the centuries.

And this is precisely what Jesus did over and over again in his ministry. The church I grew up in used to talk a great deal about "the plan of salvation," and I got the idea as a child that Jesus had one set propositional formula that he offered to everyone he met. However, as I began to read the actual accounts in the Gospels, I discovered this was not how Jesus worked. He said very different things to different people, and made a variety of demands on the individuals he encountered.

For example, when Nicodemus came to him by night and reached out for help, Jesus said, "Do you know what you need to do, Nicodemus? You need to be born again" (John 3:3). However, in the very next chapter, Jesus encountered a Samaritan woman at Jacob's well and said something utterly different to her. There was not a word about "being born again"; he spoke about her need for "living water" that could satisfy (John 4:10). Then there was the conversation Jesus had with the one known as "the rich young ruler." Jesus said yet a third different thing to this young man: "What you need to do is to sell what you have, give it to the poor, and come and follow me."

Now at first I was confused by this variety of demands and expectations. Where was the one simple "plan of salvation" I had heard so much about? However, as I reflected more deeply on each of these encounters, I began to sense that there was a common thread in all of this. While the form of Jesus' demands differed in each of these cases, the content was the same. What he was doing was taking the imperative, "Let God be God," and applying it specifically to the kind of idolatry he perceived in each of these individuals! For example, as a Pharisee and a ruler of the synagogue, Nicodemus undoubtedly prized his birth as a Jewish person more highly than any other aspect of his existence. He was a direct descendent of Abraham and Isaac and Jacob, which meant he considered himself better than all other human beings because of his physical lineage. By saying, "You must be born again," Jesus was saying, in effect, "You must give up this form of idolatry. Racial pride is not a reality that can save or fulfill a person. You must learn to love the Lord your God with all your heart and soul and mind and strength. He alone is strong enough to bear the weight of ultimate devotion. Let yourself be born into the joy of being a child of God, not just a son of Abraham."

Similarly, Jesus spoke to the Samaritan woman and the rich young ruler about the things they prized most highly—for the former, it was physical sensation and for the latter it was obviously material possessions. To each of these people Jesus offered a plan of salvation based on the unique circumstances of their lives. (After all, what would you think of a doctor who handed the same prescription to every patient who walked into his office?) But Jesus' purpose in each case was the same—to get them to let go of their devotion to false, inadequate gods and to accept the true God who alone was capable of saving them.

The question for all of us remains: Who really is our god— Is it the ones we have made or the One who made us? It's important to know, for it is only the living God of Moses who has the power to save and fulfill any of us.

21

WALKING IN THE LIGHT

1 John 1:5–7

ABRAHAM LINCOLN ONCE REMARKED that his father
had taught him the value of hard work, but had never
succeeded in teaching him to enjoy it. I find myself with
much the same sentiment when it comes to interpersonal
conflict and disagreements. To be perfectly honest, I like
it best when people relate together in warmth and harmony and affection. I agree with the psalmist: "How
good and pleasant it is when brothers dwell in unity"
(133:1, RSV). However, after fifty-two years of living, I
have come to the conclusion that such a harmonious state
is not always possible or, for that matter, even desirable,
for I have seen what happens when affability becomes a
god and "peace at any price" is sought between persons.
This does not make for relational health. In fact, what it
does is stifle the emergence of genuine individuality and
render impossible the kind of honest interaction in which
real differences are shared and true fellowship is born.
Thus, I have come to feel about conflict the way Lincoln

felt about hard work. I still cannot say I "enjoy" it, but I do see its value, and I believe that developing some philosophy about conflict and devising some mechanism of conflict-management is basic to authentic living. To that end, I believe the insights of the Bible can prove extraordinarily useful.

It helps me to remember that conflict is the inevitable corollary of individuality. If each one of us had been created exactly alike, there would be no occasion for disagreement. But obviously this is not the shape of creation; in fact, if we take seriously the doctine of the Trinity, then we see that not even God is characterized by "homogenized oneness"! There is individuality and diversity even within the Godhead—dynamic interaction between the Father and the Son and the Holy Spirit. Therefore, it is not surprising that a world created in the image of this kind of deity would be full of diversity.

This, of course, is exactly what we find. I am I and you are you; each one of us is a genuine original from the hand of God. We do not think or feel or act just alike, and this is because we were made to be different. This means there will be conflict between us when our differences interact, but it also means there will be a richness and creativity that would not be possible if we were all just the same. Conflict is the price that must be paid for individuality, and there really is no way to have the one without the other.

As a matter of fact, it is precisely through conflict and resistance that our individual natures are shaped. In other words, without conflict we would never be quite sure where we leave off and where another reality begins. Paul Tillich once defined reality as "that which we come against, that which resists us." It is precisely by encountering such resistance that a baby begins to distinguish the limits of his being. At first all the world seems to be one piece—an extension of his own body. But then

202

he pushes on the side of the crib and it does not move, or he demands something of his mother and she does not comply. By experiencing resistance to his will, he begins what the experts call "the process of individuation"; that is, he starts to realize that there are separate realities outside himself over which he has no control. This is the beginning of one individual's interaction with other individuals, and when this happens "the name of the game" is conflict. Without it, the true shape of each unique personality would never become known. Just as friction between certain types of rocks produces sparks of light, so the friction of one individual personality rubbing against another produces sparks that illuminate what each one is truly like.

There is a real sense in which I do not really know you or you me until we get to a point where we differ. As long as we agree, it is hard to distinguish what is truly unique about each of us. But when I "come up against" something in you that is not the same as what is in me, then the shape of your individuality begins to stand out clearly and distinctly over against mine. Only then is there a chance for us to have real fellowship together.

I remember quite well the time a new English teacher transferred into my high school during the middle of the term. She was the epitome of Southern warmth and graciousness, and at first she demanded little from the class. She was totally affirming; she showed an interest in each one of us and was understanding and sympathetic and pliable. In a word, she worked at identifying with us and with our concerns. Before long, certain members of the class began to take advantage of this atmosphere of permissiveness. They would be late to class or cut out altogether, and they would ignore assignment deadlines. One boy even went so far as to fail to show up for his first test, confidently assuming he would be allowed to make it up at his own convenience.

It was at this point that the teacher countered with a move of self-declaration. While still remaining warm and gracious, she proceeded to draw the line as to what would and would not be acceptable. She made it emphatically clear that classes had to be attended, assignments done, and tests taken on schedule. In the space of a few minutes she "blew the whistle" on our excesses, and by direct confrontation established her own being over against ours. It was a rather rude and painful awakening for many in the class, but in a deep sense it set the stage for a healthy teacher-pupil relationship. You see, until she resisted us, asserted her own demands over against our desires, we were actually "walking in darkness." We did not really "know" her, or how to relate to her. But once she risked the conflict that goes with confrontation and self-declaration, new possibilities developed.

This, I think, is precisely what the writer of 1 John was talking about when he affirmed that "God is light and in him is no darkness at all," which means that God is willing to be himself in all openness. He does not hide his uniqueness in darkness or shadows, but is by nature manifestly transparent. Walking "in the light, as he is in the light" means practicing the same kind of openness— doing what my teacher did by getting out on the table how she felt and what she expected so that we could negotiate realistically with her. This is the only way we can have true fellowship with one another—by openly acknowledging the realities of our various uniquenesses and then interacting in honesty and candor.

Now, to be sure, this way of relating carries with it the possibility of conflict and disagreement, because two individuals who are not the same will often come down on the opposite sides of things. But I repeat, this is the price we have to pay both for individuality and for the kind of fellowship that grows out of honest interchange. If we try at all costs to avoid conflict of this type, we will end up either stifling our individuality or missing out on real fellowship with other human beings.

I once had a minister-friend in another state who got so depressed that he had to be hospitalized and his family requested that I visit with him. When I asked him what the doctors were saying about his case, he replied that his problems seemed to be rooted in his desire to be "a pleaser." He said, "All my life I have put up a front, acted a part, pretended to think and feel things that were not really me. I would get up in the morning and put on whatever mask was expected of me that day—always agreeable, always cooperative. The doctors tell me that as a result I have virtually lost touch with my own uniqueness. I have worn so many masks for so long that I don't know who I am. This is why I am so depressed, and the only answer lies in reestablishing the shape of my own personhood. But to do that means not having everyone like me, and I simply don't know whether I can stand that kind of pain."

Never in all my life had I seen the interrelatedness of conflict and individuality more clearly stated, and in this case the mental-hospital surroundings graphically underlined the real issues that were at stake. I thought of Jesus' parable of the talents, and how it applied to this situation. The uniqueness of each of our lives is one of the things God has entrusted to us. If we accept this and acknowledge it openly as we interact with others; that is, "if we walk in the light as he is in the light," then increase and blessing will come to us as it did to the two faithful servants in the parable. But if out of fear of conflict we bury our uniqueness out of sight and never let anybody see what we really feel and think, then, like the third servant in the parable, we will lose what individuality we have. Written deep in all of life is the principle, "What you do not use you will lose," and this is as true of the unique shape of our personhood as anything else.

If the fear of conflict keeps us from being our own true selves over against others, our hiding behind false agreeable masks will result in our losing our faces altogether, and this means that something original that God thought enough of to create will be destroyed.

The other adverse consequence that comes from refusing "to walk in the light" is inability to experience authentic, reality-based fellowship. We all know what it is to try to walk through a strange place in the dark. When we do not know where things are located, the likelihood of stumbling and falling and hurting or getting hurt is much greater. The principle holds true in personal relationships. If you do not tell me honestly how you really feel and think, then I am left to stumble in darkness in relation to you, and I may well make matters worse because you have not given me the benefit of knowing the realities of the situation. This is what Eric Berne was talking about in his book, *Games People Play,* in which he describes the many forms of indirection people utilize instead of daring to "walk in the light as God is in the light." What such "games" produce is a state of unreality, a phoniness of relationship that deprives us of the enriching fellowship we could have with each other.

Some years ago I participated on the program of the Evangelistic Conference in South Carolina. During the afternoon session on the first day, a well-known preacher in our denomination gave a rousing sermon that corresponded exactly with what the audience wanted to hear, and they responded enthusiastically. After the session was over, a man whom I had known in the seminary came up to me practically boiling with rage. He asked heatedly, "Did you just hear Dr. So-and-so?" When I replied that I had, he said, "That was demagoguery if I ever saw it! That man knows better than that. He was simply playing to the grandstands and exploiting prejudice to his own advantage."

As these very words were falling from his lips, who should walk up but the very speaker about whom my friend had been expounding so strongly. I could hardly believe my eyes at what happened, for lo and behold, face to face with the man himself, my friend's expression completely changed, and he said warmly, "Good job, friend, you really rang the bell. Nice to have you in South Carolina."

After the preacher had moved on, I turned to my friend in amazement and said, "I don't believe this! One minute you are telling me you feel a certain way about a sermon and then, face to face with the preacher in question, you say the very opposite. I want to know: Which is the real you?"

He turned red in the face and said, "Well, what I said to you at first is how I really feel, but you can't just go up to a man of power like that and be perfectly honest!"

"If that is the case," I replied, "I don't think you have any right to accuse him of playing to the gallery. It appears to me that you just did to his face the very thing you accuse him of doing with the audience."

This exchange triggered a heart-to-heart discussion between the two of us. We walked back to the hotel together and talked for over an hour about the issue of conflict and integrity. I felt then—and I still feel—that what he was doing is the kind of thing that makes authentic human relationships well-nigh impossible. Had he said to this man what he really felt, there would probably have been conflict, but there might also have been light and growth.

For example, my friend might have discovered he was mistaken about this preacher—maybe he really did believe all those things that evoked amens from the crowd. Thus a truer image of the other man's reality would have emerged. On the other hand, if the preacher *had* been guilty of "playing the grandstands," my friend's recognition of what was happening and his honesty in calling the other man's hand on it might have provided a redemptive encounter. In other words, these two men might have had a moment of authentic fellowship out of which light could have come. As it was, they passed "as two ships in the night," walking in utter darkness because, out of fear of conflict, my friend had "hidden his light under a bushel" and failed to take responsibility for the way he really felt.

In my judgment this is one of the great sicknesses of our time. We have made a virtual god of affability and pleasantness when it comes to face-to-face relationships, and as a result little authentic sharing takes place. There is all the difference in the world in "the games people play" and walking "in the light as he is in the light." The price of the former is prohibitive; it stifles individuality, poisons relationships and causes us to be forever stumbling around in darkness. On the other hand, the price of "walking in the light" sometimes involves open disagreement. But, believe me, it is worth it! For when we dare to be true to ourselves and let this be openly seen, then the possibility is opened that we can have fellowship one with another, and know a richness of life that far exceeds "homogenized oneness" or strained congeniality.

Come, then—hard as it might be, let us lay aside the ways of darkness, and with courage and hope and daring let us "walk in the light as he is in the light." In that way, we can have fellowship one with another, and the blood of Jesus Christ, can cleanse us from all unrighteousness.

22

THE DELIGHT OF GOD

Philippians 2:5–11

THERE WAS A TIME IN MY LIFE when making a name for myself was exceedingly important. You see, I was never satisfied with the name I had been given. Outside of a few people in my family and neighborhood, who had ever heard of John Claypool? I was a nonentity, and that bothered me. I longed for my name to become a household word, to go down in history and to be as well-known as names like Franklin Delano Roosevelt or Winston Churchill or Dwight D. Eisenhower. If this could happen, I used to say to myself, perhaps the stigma of "nobodiness" that I have always felt could be broken. If I could just become famous, I thought, that would give me a reason to like myself and to hold up my head as really "being somebody" who had accomplished something.

This was the frame of reference in which I lived the first two-thirds of my life, and needless to say, the figure of Jesus both baffled and perplexed me at that time. Even a surface reading of the Gospels indicated that he did not share this obsession of mine for fame. In fact, it is astonishing how downright indifferent Jesus was to notoriety or reputation-building.

For example, during the early days of his ministry in Galilee, when he was making such an impact on people with the wisdom of his words and the power of his deeds, he deliberately asked those he helped not to say anything about it to other people. One day in the wilderness, after he had fed the five thousand, the crowd got so excited they wanted to make him their king, and he turned down their offer without batting an eye. There was a time when I was a little child that I used to fantasize about being "president of the world." That is what I would say under my breath when people asked me what I wanted to be when I grew up. I envisioned the whole human race in one vast pyramid with one place of preeminence at the top and me in that place! Thus, I could not understand how Jesus could be so indifferent to what seemed so important to me.

Or then again, there was the last evening of his life. Just that afternoon the disciples had been quarreling about this very issue of "making names for themselves" and over who was going to be the greatest and all that. They were playing one of humanity's oldest games— "King of the Mountain"—and had gotten so competitive with each other that when they gathered for supper in the Upper Room no one was willing to lower himself to do the servant task of washing the others' feet. It was a tense moment, but then John's Gospel says, "Jesus, knowing that the Father had given all things into his hands, and that he had come from God and was going to God, rose from supper, laid aside his garments, and girded himself with a towel. Then he poured water into a basin and began to wash the disciples' feet" (13:3–5).

In other words, Jesus did not hold himself above doing the most lowly sort of work. He cared not one whit for status or rank or prestige. And then, too, there is that baffling phrase Paul uses: "He made himself of no reputation." During the days when I was trying by every means possible to make a name for myself, I used to puzzle over those words and wonder again and again how Jesus could be that way and why something that was so important to my existence could be so unimportant to him.

And yet precisely at this point, I believe, lies one of the revolutionary secrets of the Christian Gospel. Why was Jesus so unconcerned to make a name for himself? How did he get to the place where he had himself off his hands so sufficiently that he was more concerned about doing something rather than just being something? I believe the answer lies farther down in the same passage. It centers in the fact that God had given his Son a name—a very special name, an utterly unique name—and that Jesus accepted that gift wholeheartedly! When I am speaking of a name here, I am using the term in the Hebraic sense of standing for the whole reality of the person. For Jesus to accept and be satisfied with his name means that he totally accepted what he was and when he was and where he was in history. He looked on the event of his own creation the very same way God did.

Do you remember how the book of Genesis describes the moment of creation? It has God saying ecstatically, "It is good! It is good! It is very, very good!" It was this radical acceptance of his name—that is, of all he had been given by the Father—that freed Jesus from having to make a name for himself and spend his energy trying to earn what he had already been given. From the very beginning Jesus was at one with the thing the Father had done for him in creation and, according to William McElvaney, this was one of the secrets to his power.

"After all," McElvaney says, "Jesus' authority among men was not because of an unusual I.Q. or mystical otherworldliness or even a winsome personality. Nor was it economic, social or political power. In part, at least, his incredible authority lay in his freedom to say: 'Life as it is given is good!' This means that it was good that Jesus' parents were who they were. It was good that his life was in the time of history that it was in. It was good that he was a male Jew. It was good that he was a carpenter, that he got to associate with the kinds of people who lived in Nazareth. All the things God had at his disposal in making him were acknowledged as good, and this accounts for the incredible trust and freedom of his life."

Jesus was able to say, "Thy will be done," at the end of his life on earth because he had come to believe that from the very beginning God's will for him was utterly good and could be trusted. Therefore, he was free to throw reputation to the winds and do the most menial sort of tasks—even washing feet. Why? Because, as the Gospel says, he knew "the Father had given all things into his hands." He knew where he came from and where he was going and who the Source of his true value was. Therefore, he was not driven by some sense of "nobodiness" to make a name for himself. He had already been given a name, a name above every name as far as God was concerned, and it was because he accepted that primal gift and proceeded to build his life upon it that Jesus was what he was.

This is the truth that every one of us needs to hear, for unless I am badly mistaken, this is a place where most of us have problems. Put in a nutshell, most of the people I have known do not like what they are or when they are or where they have been placed in history. Their quarrel with God goes all the way back to the beginning, to the very first thing he ever did for them—the act of creating them. They do not like the particular set of gifts or capacities he has given them; they resent the place in history into which he inserted them and the kinds of experiences that surrounded their early days.